AGAINST ALL ODDS

Your Student's Life Journey With Autism

An Educator's Guide to Autism

AGAINST ALL ODDS

Your Student's Life Journey With Autism

An Educator's Guide to Autism

CAROL BASILE, Ph.D.

Mother, Teacher, School Psychologist

Copyright © 2023 *Dragon Gate Media*

All rights reserved. No part of this publication may be reproduced, distributed, or transmitted in any form or by any means, including photocopying, recording, or other electronic or mechanical methods, without the prior written permission of the publisher, except in the case of brief quotations embodied in reviews.

www.dragongatemedia.com

ISBN: 979-8-9853734-7-9 softcover
ISBN: 979-8-9853734-8-6 e-book

Special discounts are available on quantity purchases.
For details, contact: 949-514-1061.

Table of Contents

Preface vii
Dedication ix
Acknowledgments xi
Prologue xiii
Introduction xv

Section One 1
Chapter 1 Autism and Unconditional Love 3
Chapter 2 Beginning to Understand 13
Chapter 3 Revenge of the Refrigerator Mom 17
Chapter 4 All in the Same Boat 21
Chapter 5 Theories that Changed My Life 27

Section Two 47
Chapter 6 Joe Finally Sleeps 49
Chapter 7 Joe Explores 65
Chapter 8 Joe's Adventures Begin 75
Chapter 9 Joe Knows Stranger Danger 85
Chapter 10 Joe Becomes a Teacher 95
Chapter 11 Joe Says "Coffee with Cocoa, Please" 107
Chapter 12 Joe Begins to Step Out of His Inner World ... 117
Chapter 13 Joe Goes Against All Odds 129
Chapter 14 Joe Goes Against All Odds Again 145
Chapter 15 Joe Steps Out on His Own 157

Section Three 169
Chapter 16 The Brighter Future 171
Chapter 17 The Purple Horse 179
Epilogue 185

Preface

Against All Odds
Your Student's Life Journey with Autism

Against All Odds: Your Student's Life Journey With Autism is the story of my son, Joe, and I as we journey through life reveling in the superpowers of Autism while coping with challenges autism characteristics can present. Joe, who, with courage and determination, struggles through life stages, far surpasses society's expectations earning a master's degree.

This is a story of taking advantage of opportunities, achieving goals, and never giving up.

This edition of Against All Odds, as in the original edition, includes what I learned to help my child overcome the difficulties of Autism while living in a world that knew little of Autism. It also includes a new chapter discussing people, on the *autism spectrum*, who have changed the world because of their unique *autistic superpowers*.

Against All Odds is a guide to assist educators in understanding family dynamics and the developmental goals of each stage of life including adaptations of theories for autistic students. It is through this understanding that true assistance can be given to autistic individuals so that they may reach their individual potential and personal goals.

Dedication

This book is dedicated to my son, Joe, who is the most courageous person I know. Joe has encountered every stage of his life with determination and quiet strength. He has strived to achieve difficult goals not only through hard work but also, with incredible persistence. Joe has achieved his goals *against all odds*.

Acknowledgments

I thank my son, Joe, who has enabled me to become the person I was meant to be. For this, I am so grateful. I especially want to thank my husband, John, who has supported and encouraged me in every endeavor. I thank John for his love and caring not only for me but also for Joe. I thank him for his insight, his thoughtful suggestions, and his incredible patience. John is the stepfather every mother dreams to have for her child. I thank John not only for being the wonderful person he is but also for sharing his wonder with Joe and me. To my dear friend, Vera, who helped me put into words what is in my heart. I thank the many loving and caring people who have helped and supported me through this incredible journey with Joe. I am immensely grateful for the friends, teachers, co-workers who have, over the years, noticed my struggles and stood with me, supporting, and encouraging me to continue.

Prologue

The Cracked Pot

A Story for Anyone Who's Not Quite Perfect

A water bearer in India had two large pots that she carried across her neck on the ends of a pole. One of the pots had a crack. While the other pot was perfect and always contained a full portion of water, the cracked pot arrived only half full by the end of her long walk from the stream to the mistress' house. This went on for two years with the bearer delivering only one-and-a-half pots of water at a time to her mistress' house.

The perfect pot was proud of its accomplishments achieving the end for which it was made. But the poor cracked pot was ashamed of its imperfection and miserable that it was able to accomplish only half of what it had been made to do. After what it perceived to be a bitter failure, it spoke to the water bearer one day by the stream. "I am ashamed of myself, and I want to apologize to you." "Why?" asked the bearer. "What are you ashamed of?" "I have been able for these past two years to deliver only half my load because this crack in my side causes water to leak out all the way back to your mistress' house. Because of my flaws, you have to do all of this work, and you don't get the full value from your efforts," the pot said. The water bearer felt sorry for the old cracked pot, and in her compassion she said, "As we return to the mistress' house, I want you to notice the beautiful flowers along the path." As they went up the hill, the old cracked pot took notice of the sun warming the beautiful wildflowers on the side of the path, and this cheered it a bit. But at the end of the trail, it still felt bad because it had leaked out half its load, and so again it apologized to the bearer for its failure. The bearer said to the pot, "Did you notice that there were flowers only on your side of the path but not on the other pot's side? "That's because I have always known about your flaw, and I took advantage of it. I planted flower seeds on your side of the path, and every day while we walked back from the stream, you've watered them," the bearer said. "For two years, I have been able to pick these beautiful flowers to decorate my mistress' table. Without you being just the way you are, she would not have this beauty to grace her house."

Moral

Each of us has our own unique flaws. We're all cracked pots. But it's the cracks and flaws that make our lives together so very interesting and rewarding. We just have to accept each person for who they are and look for the good in them.

Introduction

From Italy to Holland: A Special Gift

Beginning A Journey

On A Journey

Six months after my husband and I were married, I became pregnant. We were basically newlyweds, but we anticipated and looked forward to life with many children. Family and friends were having babies, and I barely could wait to join them in what I considered to be our new stage of life. However, fate intervened and my life turned out to be very different from theirs.

The following is a short story taken from a "Dear Abby" column that sums up exactly what I felt after the birth of my son.

WELCOME TO HOLLAND by Emily Perl Kingsley

I am often asked to describe the experience of raising a child with a disability—to try to help people who have not shared the unique experience to understand it, to imagine how it would feel. It's like this...When you're going to have a baby, it's like planning a fabulous vacation trip—to Italy. You buy a bunch of guidebooks and make your wonderful plans. The Coliseum. Michelangelo's David. The gondolas in Venice. You may learn some handy phrases in Italian. It's all very exciting. After months of eager anticipation, the day finally arrives. You pack your bags and off you go. Several hours later, the plane lands. The flight attendant comes and says, "Welcome to Holland." "Holland?!" you say. "What do you mean, Holland? I signed up for Italy! I'm supposed to be in Italy. All my life I've dreamed of going to Italy." "But there's been a change in the flight plan. They've landed in Holland and there you must stay." The important thing is that they haven't taken you to a horrible, disgusting, filthy place full of pestilence, famine, and disease. It's just a different place. So, you must go out and buy new guidebooks. You must learn a whole new language. And you will meet a whole new group of people you would never have met. It's just a different place. It's slower paced than Italy, less flashy than Italy. But after you've been there for a while and you catch your breath, you look around, and you begin to notice that Holland has windmills, Holland has tulips, Holland even has Rembrandts.

But everyone you know is busy coming and going from Italy, and they're all bragging about what a wonderful time they had there. And for the rest of your life, you will say, "Yes, that's where I was supposed to go. That's what I had planned." And the pain of that will never, ever, ever go away because the loss of that dream is a very significant loss. But if you spend your life mourning the fact that you didn't get to Italy, you may never be free to enjoy the very special, the very lovely things about Holland.

Most of us believe that expecting a child, especially our first child, is a great gift. We anticipate it with elation and some trepidation. We are on the threshold of an adventure of a lifetime. This adventure holds many surprises, both happy and exciting, and distressing and disappointing. However, most expectant parents plunge into parenthood with the greatest of hopes, knowing our lives will change but not knowing how much of a change to expect. When I was expecting my son, Joe, I had similar hopes and dreams like every other expectant parent. I believed I was ready for my journey as a parent, and I was ready to change my life as much as any other mother. What I didn't expect or plan for was a journey into the complete unknown. I didn't expect to change as much as I needed to change. However, the change created a new me - a me that, I believe with all my heart, was always meant to be.

MY GREATEST GIFT

On July 12, 1966, I received the greatest gift that can be given to a mother. The gift is my son, Joe.

Joe changed my life for the better in so many ways. He truly is a gift. He was a wonderful child, so eager to learn, quiet and happy in his own world. He now is a wonderful adult, thoughtful, loving, and intelligent. He is autistic.

He was diagnosed with autism at six years old in 1973, the Dark Ages of Autism. And believe me, those were dark years. When Joe was seven, his neurologist advised me to put Joe into an institution because, "He will not be able to accomplish anything In his life." The neurologist said Joe actually would be better off in an institution and I could then, "go on with my life." I was horrified and devastated by what I heard. Joe is my only child. He is the only child I would ever be able to have. Against the advice of doctors and educators, I decided to keep Joe at home and go on with my life with him in it. It was the best decision because it changed my life completely and for the better - so much better. Joe is truly the best thing that has ever happened to me. I say that without reservation, even when considering struggles that were intense at times. I became the person I am because of him. I do what I do professionally today because of him. Joe helped me to become the best me I could ever possibly become. My hope is that I did the same for him.

Joe taught me patience and tolerance. He taught me to appreciate the differences in people and to value those differences. He taught me to see the uniqueness of each individual and to value that uniqueness. Over the years, I have become more tolerant and patient with my own uniqueness and view it as an asset. Joe has given me myself. He has given me a life worth living.

How did Joe change my life? Well, let me count the ways. Because of his autism, he presented unique parenting problems I needed to resolve. I found a strength within myself that I otherwise may not have known I had.

He turned me into a keen observer of human behavior, but perhaps most importantly is that he helped me accept differences in others and in myself.

When Joe was in kindergarten, I had the opportunity to volunteer at his school helping the teacher in the classroom and reading stories to children in the library. I think the teachers were happy to have me as a volunteer since they didn't know what to do with Joe. They struggled to cope with him. He was an interesting child to me but not so much to his teachers. Soon after my first-year volunteering, the principal offered me a job in the school's learning center. The principal said to me that he liked the way I worked with at-risk children in the school. Without a moment's hesitation, I took the job and loved every minute of it. I realized I was good at helping children with learning problems and behavioral difficulties because I had learned patience and tolerance from Joe. After being on the job for a year or so, the principal and several teachers suggested I begin to take college courses with the intention of becoming a teacher. Becoming a teacher had been a secret dream of mine for as long as I can remember. Due to financial constraints, it was a dream I believed would never come true. But the almost constant urging from the school's Learning Center director led me to begin to take college courses. Not only did I want to become a teacher, I wanted to learn more about autism, learning disabilities, and behavioral problems. If the doctors and educators could not help Joe, I would go to school and learn how to help him myself. To be fair, there was no real research on autism at that time, and doctors and educators didn't know what to do with children experiencing social differences.

These were the Dark Ages of Autism. That was the beginning of many life changes—major life changes. College courses helped me to realize that I did not cause Joe's autism, which actually was a fear of mine due to theories at that time blaming mothers for autistic characteristics in their children. The subjects I studied helped me to realize I was doing the best I could as a mother. Could I have done better? In hindsight, yes. I just did not know how at the time. Because of my desire to understand Joe and help him and others like him, I continued my education and completed my bachelor's degree in education with minors in psychology, special education, and science. After attaining my first full-time teaching position at a middle school in a neighboring city, I immediately went back to college to acquire special education credentials to go with my regular classroom teaching credentials. By this time, I was a single mother. Unfortunately, Joe's dad could not deal with his son's autism, and he began to drink heavily. It was extremely sad and difficult but actually, looking back, I think it was the best resolution for all of us. At that time, the problems associated with having a disabled child broke up marriages because professionals did not know how to help the child or the family. I believe that situation has changed with worthwhile and helpful therapies such as Applied Behavior Analysis. Still, it is not easy today but there is more support now than there was in the '60s and '70s when I began my journey.

After I finished my special education courses, I returned to college for a master's degree in counseling psychology and became a high school counselor. I worked full time as a high school counselor and worked part time in an animal hospital to keep a roof over our heads, food in our mouths and to pay my graduate school tuition. Joe did better in high school than anyone thought possible. We were busy with school and work responsibilities. Life was going well.

I currently teach psychology at a local community college. I've worked for many years at a clinic facilitating groups of adolescents released from juvenile hall, adults with anger issues, and parents experiencing difficult divorces or who have lost their children to social services and want the children returned to them. Most of my clients are ordered by the court to attend my groups. They are people hurting and in need. I know the feeling.

They are me. Even though life could be difficult given Joe's schooling and our tight finances, we usually had fun talking about our days, reading together, and watching old movies. We worked through immense problems both at school and at home and survived. Joe did well despite all the problems we encountered with the schools. He graduated elementary school, even though we were told by educators and psychologists he would not be able to accomplish that. He graduated high school with the President's Academic Fitness Award. (I knew he was intelligent!) He graduated college with a bachelor's degree in history and a minor in geography. He went on to achieve a master's degree in political science. In college, Joe tutored international students and worked in a university library.

I am so happy I did not put him in an institution. His life is not only valuable to me but also to the others he has helped.

In the chapters to come, I share my story and what I did to make our lives better and easier. Many of the ideas and activities are similar to what professionals use with autistic children today. Some are not. Some of the methods I used are uniquely mine because they worked for Joe. In separate sections at the end of chapters, I share insights and provide some suggestions that are helpful to parents. Here are lessons I have learned over 55 years with an autistic son. My hope is that you see value in our story and use our story to assist you in helping your students reach their potential.

Section One

Family Life in Relation to an Autistic Child: Rearing with a Twist

CHAPTER 1

Autism and Unconditional Love

The Gift We Give Ourselves

The Gift Keeps Giving

Unconditional love is the greatest gift that we can give to anyone. The interesting truth regarding unconditional love is that when we give it, we also receive it. In essence, it is the greatest gift we can give to ourselves.

Giving our children unconditional love lays the foundation for a special parent/child relationship that is the most unique relationship in all of humanity. Giving our students Unconditional positive regard develops a powerful teacher/student relationship. Unconditional regard for someone who is different or who behaves differently may be difficult at times but it is astonishingly rewarding. Unconditional regard is the foundation for our main goal of helping people with autism to live happy, productive, satisfying lives. Considering this goal, it is important to understand and accept each autistic person as the individual he/she truly <u>is</u>, including their personality, temperament, physical, mental and social abilities, their interests, and the problems they may encounter at school, in the workplace, and in the community at large. As humans, we tend to categorize people as a means of expediting action. Given the span of abilities on the autism spectrum, we cannot just group autistic people in one lump. We are forced to understand and work with each autistic person as an individual. This is a good thing. This is the way we need to work with everyone, anyway. With autism, however, we must consider each autistic person as an individual with certain needs, abilities, and goals in life. Each deserves encouragement, support, and unconditional love.

Parents Vital Role
Children look to their parents for food, clothing, shelter, love, and acceptance. As children, we also look to our parents for self-understanding, self-esteem, and personal value. This is vital to the development of a child, and autistic children are no different. Autistic infants and children still need love and acceptance. They also need a sense of self-esteem and personal worth, even though their lack of normal response may hamper their interactions and relationships. These needs are still true and very real in their lives.
Whitney Houston's, "The Greatest Love of All" is such a beautiful song with a valuable message. In the song, she says that the greatest love that any of us could have is to love ourselves. She then goes on to sing that loving ourselves is easy to achieve.

Is It Really So Easy?
It is widely believed that to love others, one must first love oneself. Although I agree that loving yourself is one of the greatest if not the greatest love, there are conditions that may not make it so easy to achieve self-love, especially if you are different from others. Autistic infants and children do not

respond to others as non-autistic infants and children do. Autistic infants and children are uncomfortable with consistent eye contact and have difficulty interpreting facial expressions. Therefore, parents, caregivers, and teachers of autistic infants and children need to make a conscious effort to interact with the autistic infant and child not only with facial expressions and eye contact but also with light touches and calm tones of voice.

The Looking Glass
There is a theory in sociology called, "The Looking-Glass Self" developed by George Cooley. This theory explains that the beliefs we have about ourselves, especially when we are young, are actually reflections of the beliefs others have about us - the looking glass. Ideally, parents love their children unconditionally, no strings attached. Unfortunately, this is not true in many families whether the family has an autistic child or not.

Over the years counseling adolescents and adults at the clinic, I learned that sometimes life situations prevent parents from expressing love to their children. It could be due to the personality of the parent or a past trauma the parent has experienced. Whatever the cause, children who don't experience unconditional love have difficulty loving themselves. Parents, caregivers, and teachers of autistic infants and children need to continuously make conscious efforts to provide children with a sense of unconditional love/regard and a sense of value.

What We Can Do
Autistic babies may have difficulty responding to others which can hinder their developing relationships, even with their parents. Developing a parent-child relationship involves several

factors: The parent's personality, temperament, and ability to parent. Of course, we need to consider the baby's temperament, personality, and manner of responding to others.

Relationships can be accomplished through loving interactions, mirroring positive facial expressions, accepting behaviors, and caressing tones of voice.

Joe had a difficult experience with his father. After Joe was diagnosed, his father rarely spoke to him. Joe's father could not accept the fact that his only child had a disorder, one that most people did not understand at all. He found it easier to ignore the problem by ignoring his son. There are a variety of reasons why a parent may have difficulty accepting a child with a disability. Many are overwhelmed with the idea of having a special needs child. That may have been the case with Joe's father. Whatever the reason, Joe basically grew up without a father.

Types of Babies

There are three types of babies and I really wish I had been aware of these types when Joe was an infant. It would have helped me to better understand Joe and his different behaviors, such as not sleeping or not wanting to be touched. I emotionally beat myself up because, not understanding, I took responsibility for all of them. I didn't know why Joe would not sleep. I didn't know why Joe behaved as he did but I truly believed that his behavior was somehow my fault. Autistic infants may have sensitive nerve endings in their skin so touching and cuddling can be painful. Autistic infants also can be overwhelmed by sounds and odors in their environment that can make it difficult for them to settle down and fall asleep well. If I had known this when Joe was an infant, I would have had a more relaxed experience with him. I hope that today's pediatricians and therapists are better able to recognize characteristics of autism in infancy so parents are not confused by differences in their infant's behavior.

The "Easy" Baby

The first type of baby is the "easy" baby. We all want an easy baby, believe me. This is the type of baby we all dream of having when we first learn we are pregnant. "Easy" babies smile a lot, eat well, sleep well, and seem happy.

With "easy" babies, we believe ourselves to be good parents. After all, we must be doing something right for our baby to be happy, well-adjusted, and smiling most of the time.

The "Slow to Warm Up" Baby

The second type of baby is the "slow to warm up" baby. This type of baby is not difficult to deal with once parents realize the baby needs time to adjust to changes. An example of a "slow to warm up" baby would be, feeding the baby a new food. You put a small spoonful of new food in the baby's mouth and when the baby realizes it has a different taste, the baby pushes it out of its mouth and allows it to run down its chin. Then, after a moment, the baby sticks out its tongue and slowly tastes the new food. After a few seconds, the baby will accept the second spoonful of the new food. The baby is now comfortable with the new food. Parents still feel good about their skills as parents because the baby eventually eats and sleeps well and will smile once he/she is comfortable with anything new. Ah, the smile. The one thing that can melt our hearts in a flash and validate our worth.

The "Difficult" Baby

The third type of baby is the one parents dread: The "difficult" baby. This type of baby might have a physical problem that causes discomfort—colic, for example. This baby does not sleep well, can be a picky eater, and may cry quite often. The difficult baby will, many times, spit new food out of its mouth instead of eating it or slowly tasting it. With this type of baby, parents don't know what they are doing wrong. Parents try to achieve the smile that they long for. That heart-melting expression with this baby is difficult to attain. Being unable to comfort a baby or not having a baby smile discourages parents. It also can affect the developing relationship between parent and baby. These temperament types follow a child into the classroom.

Strained Relationship
Unfortunately, many times the relationship between parents and the difficult baby is strained. That strained relationship may continue into childhood and adulthood, robbing both parent and child of a potentially great relationship. Some babies fall in this category due to the physical discomfort they feel when withdrawing from drugs in a pregnant mother's system. Autistic babies also can fall into this category because of their difficulty interpreting facial expressions, not wanting to be touched, and being stressed by sounds and odors. Of course, the discomfort felt on the part of the autistic infant when touched hampers a developing relationship as parents want and feel a need to hold and cuddle their infants. Humans don't just need love; we need unconditional love. As children grow and develop, they need to know that their parents and teachers love them no matter what.

Mirroring Unconditional Love
Unconditional love is imperative for children to grow up and love themselves and to feel self-esteem and self-worth. As the parent looks on at a child with love, the love is absorbed by the child and

is then reflected back. Unconditional love is the basis of the "Greatest Love of All." Every child deserves it. Not every child receives it.

The Challenges: Expectations
Unconditional love can be challenging for parents of autistic infants since developing a parent/child relationship can be difficult. Most autistic children do not respond in the same way as children who are not autistic. They often don't smile as expected or enjoy being held. Relationships are developed through give-and-take and responding to each other in somewhat expected ways. Parents need to know they are good parents. Most parents look to their children for that reassurance. If the baby is happy and smiles, parents are happy and feel secure in their parenting skills. If the baby is not responding with smiles and apparent happiness, parents feel they are less than stellar parents. We continue to try to develop a relationship but the autistic baby does not respond in ways that lead us to believe that we are good parents. This can be detrimental to developing not only a good relationship with the child but also to assessing our parenting skills in a realistic light. These autistic infant characteristics may have been a factor in Joe's father being able to ignore Joe after the diagnosis. He had not developed a satisfactory relationship with Joe due to Joe's inability to react in expected ways. Joe's father never seemed to develop the type of relationship that allowed him to overcome his son's behavior. The very first objective as a parent of an autistic child is to love him or her unconditionally. That, ultimately, is the most important aspect of parenting.

It Takes Time

Developing a relationship with an autistic infant means being gentle with your child, smiling even though you might not get a smile back, and hugging even though you might not be hugged back. It's important to keep showing and expressing love and approval to our autistic children.

As soon as Joe could tolerate touch, I hugged him often. I took his little arms and put them around me and gave myself a little squeeze with his arms. I just kept doing this year after year. I believed that if I kept mimicking hugging, Joe would know he was loved and would eventually learn to hug back. Joe did learn to put his arms on my shoulders when I hugged him.

Then, one day as I hugged Joe and he had put his hands on my shoulders, I felt a little squeeze from him. Oh, is this real? Is this a hug? Yes, it was. I finally got my hug. It took 42 years, but I got it. When I hug Joe now, he mostly keeps his arms on my shoulders. Yet, every once in a while when I hug him, Joe will put his arms around me and give a little squeeze. My heart sings.

An Instruction Manual?

Unfortunately, babies don't come with an instruction manual. That would be so helpful, especially for a first child. I remember coming home from the hospital and putting Joe in the crib and immediately thinking somewhat in a panic, "What do I do now?" In retrospect, I have learned a lot since my son was born. Most of what I did with him as a baby was basically flying by the seat of my pants. I know all parents feel that way, but when you slowly begin to realize that your child is not like "normal" children and you don't have anyone to talk to about it, you really feel like there is no plan to follow and no role model available. I made many mistakes, but there were many things that I did right - theoretically, that is. The one thing that I know I did right was love him, unconditionally.

So often I wish I could do this parenting "thing" all over again with what I know now, NOT what I knew then. I hope by writing this book I may help others who find themselves in the remarkable position of teaching and learning from an autistic child.

The above family background is the chain of events many of your autistic students and their parents have experienced before they reach your classroom.

CHAPTER 2

Beginning to Understand

Knowledge is Power

Walk Out of the Fog

Knowledge helped me find my way out of the fog of the Dark Ages of Autism. Learning about child development and brain development enabled me to be a better parent to my child. Child development theories help in understanding students with autism. **Seek the knowledge and walk out of the fog.**

College Bound

As an older student (I was 30 years old when I took my first college course) with a special needs child and working with special needs children in a learning center. I could study and observe Joe and my students to see how what I was learning, played out in real life which enabled me to engage in a truly incredible learning experience.

Infant Medical Information

While I was studying special education and completing my internships, I came upon some interesting information. One of the most useful items was to discover that every child in special education classes needs to have an IEP, an *Individualized Education Plan*. To complete the intake of information about the child for the IEP, a medical history is necessary. That's where it became very interesting for me.

Every special needs child I've worked with had some kind of medical difficulty in the first year of life. Most had high fevers, ear infections, colic, and/or difficulty falling asleep. Some of the mothers experienced very difficult births—early delivery, late delivery, long labor, and complications during the labor and delivery. There seemed to be a pattern here.

Not every child had experienced these problematic situations in infancy, but I heard enough of these stories to warrant a closer look into their consequences and later diagnosis of autism or other learning disabilities.

<u>It Gets Personal</u>

I experienced a long, difficult labor due to what is now known as preeclampsia. Joe's heartbeat was undetectable for two to three hours before birth. He was alive but traumatized. In infancy, Joe had high fevers, earaches, colic, and extreme difficulty falling asleep. Given that personal history, I began to pay close attention to this information when taking medical histories for the IEPs.

Making Connections

It seemed to me that something was affecting the brain development of these children. We were so often seeing the consequences of infant medical problems showing up later in schools but not so much in the doctors' offices. So often, doctors tell parents after a difficult birth that the children are perfectly normal. Well, that is true to a certain extent. Most doctors don't tell the parents to be on the alert for symptoms of possible later academic or social problems.

Now, I realize that no doctor wants to crush the hopes and dreams of new parents. However, I believe that some information about possible side effects from medical issues at birth and in infancy should be required. It is so much better if parents know what to look for as far as possible symptoms of autism or a learning disability.

Doctors can tell parents to be alert if their infant experiences high fevers or has difficulty sleeping. Parents need to be aware of inconsistent eye contact or lack of interaction. We know that early diagnosis and treatment helps the child so much more than when the diagnosis comes later in the child's life. Joe is my only child and for good reason: the pregnancy was riddled with difficulties. During his first year of life, Joe had high fevers, ear infections, flu, and colic. These seemed to be precursors of later problems: dislike of physical touch and a need to organize his toys, both of which happen to be characteristics of autism.

Doctors and These Connections

Neither doctors nor educational professionals saw the connection between these medical problems in infancy and later educational and social problems. We now know there is a connection, and research is ongoing. A few years later when I was studying special education, I started to think about Joe's birth and the labor and delivery
problems surrounding his birth. Things began to make sense to me. I have to admit I wish our doctors had made this connection years earlier, but better late than never.

Out of the Fog

When Joe was an infant and later as a child in school, I felt so inadequate. I was frustrated and felt like I was walking in a fog. No one was there to help me or even to understand what was going on with us. Now, thanks to more than five decades of experience with Joe and an education that gave me much needed information, I feel more capable and so much more able to deal with the problematic situations I face with Joe and others like him. It has been very satisfying to be able to use my experiences, good and bad, successful, and unsuccessful, to help others. This is one of the precious gifts given to me by Joe. This is the gift I share with educators.

Chapter 3

Revenge of the Refrigerator Mom

Long-Awaited Affirmation

Lack of Information

In the so-called Dark Ages of Autism, doctors, psychologists, and theorists tried to explain autism and its characteristics based on the little knowledge they had. At the time, science had not made much progress in explaining autism. The professionals tried to explain away its strange characteristics, but they were not too successful given the lack of understanding of brain development at the time. As my son's neurologist told me, "We know more about outer space than we know about the brain." That was unsettling, to say the least.

The Refrigerator Mom

At the time, there was a popular theory that blamed mothers for causing autistic traits in their children by being emotionally cold. Most, if not all, present-day theorists dispute this theory. At the time it hurt mothers of autistic children, including me.

After Joe's autism diagnosis and my refusal to place him in an institution, I realized quickly that there was really no one to guide me once I made the decision to raise my son. I searched for reasons for his autistic behavior and what I was doing wrong. I berated myself as a mother and as a person and allowed everyone else to do the same, including my son's father, my husband at the time. Joe's father would scream at me that I was the cause of Joe's problems. He threatened to divorce me and take Joe away from me. He told me that he would make sure that I would never see Joe again. I accepted all this criticism as reality and lived in fear that Joe would be taken from me. The core of my being was devastated but I continued to do what I believed best for Joe. I was his mother.

Joe's Unseen Characteristics
I knew Joe was different, but what I saw was not his disability. I saw incredible intelligence. Joe's memory was flawless. He taught himself to read. He could draw maps of the world from memory and state the population and natural resources of each country. In my mind, Joe was not disabled but exceptional.
Joe learned easily and quickly needing new things and experiences at regular intervals. He learned his letters in days and was able to organize his room according to the alphabet. He could complete picture puzzles in minutes, actually completed these puzzles face down by just looking at the shapes of the puzzle pieces. He loved to learn. He was an information sponge in infancy and beyond. Why did no one else see this? Despite all of the remarkable things Joe could do, Joe's teachers and school psychologist continued to accuse me of being in denial about his problems at school. I was not in denial regarding Joe's differences and inability to function normally in the classroom. I just focused on his incredible abilities that the school professionals

consistently ignored. They completely disregarded Joe's interests, which would otherwise have enabled them to enter Joe's world and begin a relationship with him.

I was not the one in denial. I used Joe's interests and abilities to reach him, to teach him, and to have a relationship with him. They ignored it all and just wanted him to be "normal" in the classroom. Joe's behavior was different from other children and nothing I did changed it.

The Long-Awaited Affirmation

When Joe was re-diagnosed at age 30, I flinched when a doctor at UCLA told me he wanted to tell me something about how I raised Joe. I remember that day as if it was yesterday. I walked into a tidy, old-fashioned office and sat in a chair next to the doctor's desk. I was so nervous that I could barely breathe. I clenched my fists and felt lightheaded. I wanted to get up and run away. I truly couldn't bear another accusation of bad mothering hurled at me. After so many years and all of Joe's accomplishments, I still prepared myself for a blow that I believed would come my way.

The doctor sat next to me and looked me right in the eye. He smiled, which confused me. He quietly said that I had done a wonderful job with Joe. He told me that I should be proud.

Well!!! I couldn't believe what I was hearing, what was happening. Was I dreaming the dream I had so longed for? I couldn't say a word. I was speechless. (Speechless is a rare thing for me. No one I know would ever describe me as speechless.) However, at that moment I just sat there, unable to say a word. As I slowly began to breathe, the tears ran down my cheeks. I couldn't help it. I was relieved, happy, and completely astonished all at the same time. The doctor smiled again and clasped my hand. The expression on his face told me he knew exactly what I was feeling. I waited 30 years for this affirmation as a mother.

As a mother of an autistic son and an educator, I realize the importance of affirming parents with whom I work. I begin my meetings with positive comments regarding their child, then proceed to the areas of struggle. To provide hope, I always present ideas for easing the child's struggles including what can be done at home. I want parents to know we are a team working for their child's benefit. As a mother, this process relieved my fears. As an educator, I remember and follow the process.

CHAPTER 4 21

All in the Same Boat

Parents of an Autistic Child

Unique Experiences but Same Expectations
Parents of autistic infants have the same expectations for their infants as other parents but often their expectations do not become realities. As parents of autistic infants, we eventually develop a different set of expectations, not bad just different. Parents of autistic children experience life a little differently than do parents of non-autistic children. The understanding or misunderstanding of autism and its characteristics can make or break family relationships. Members of our family did not understand Joe and his behavior. We were excluded from many family functions. Unfortunately, many relatives still, to this day, don't understand his behavior. Some want to understand. Some don't even try to understand.

Building Relationships
Relationships are challenging. They require communication, understanding, honesty and trust. All are components vital for a solid relationship. Developing a relationship with an autistic

infant can be challenging but incredibly satisfying. Infants need a trustworthy caregiver, and learn to trust through the consistent satisfaction of their needs. Infants learn love from a gentle touch. How infants respond to their parents' actions will help or hinder the developing relationship. Joe's responses to my actions were different from his cousin, who responded to sound and touch by smiling and reaching out his little arms. Joe just stared at me for a few seconds and proceeded to turn his head. He rarely reached out toward me or in the direction of my voice.

Many parents of autistic babies believe their babies don't like them or that they are doing something wrong. I have heard this so often. These false impressions impact our attachment between us and our child.

Attachments are the foundation or building block of a parent-child relationship. As difficult as it may be, parents of autistic babies still need to interact with their babies and respond to their cries, despite the fact they may not receive the same responses as parents of non-autistic infants.

Interaction between parent and baby is perhaps even more necessary for the security and well-being of the autistic baby.

It's Personal

My son did not offer much eye contact nor did he like to be touched, much less held. He did not smile much and seemed uncomfortable outside his own world. As he became more accustomed to my touch, he protested less. Initially, I was devastated by the thought that he did not like me. As a new mother, I wanted everything to be absolutely perfect. I wanted him to smile at me. I so wanted to cuddle with him. In reality, nothing was perfect. I did everything I could to soothe him and make him comfortable with touch. I literally spent hours bending over his crib, lightly stroking his forehead and cheek to soothe and accustom him to my touch.

As he grew older, Joe became tolerant of touch though not happy about it. I changed my behavior to reflect his comfort levels. He cried less that way. I did not force issues like sleep times. Although that might seem irresponsible to the outside world, I thought it was best because Joe seemed so much happier with his natural rhythms.

I had one cousin, Marguerite, who had six children. She really understood the different personalities of children. She suspected that Joe was different, and it was fine with her. She was the only one who encouraged me as a mother and helped me in later years with Joe by giving Joe the opportunity to learn to talk on the phone, among other kind and wonderful things. She helped me to begin to feel like a worthwhile and competent mother. Every parent needs to have a special person like her in their lives, especially when parenting a special needs child. She helped me to believe in myself.

Joe's Continued Differences

As time went on, I realized I needed to interact with Joe in ways he could tolerate. He loved to do repetitive behaviors that are a hallmark of autism. He twirled small flowers in his hands. He did this for hours. If someone took them away from him, he acted as if his world ended. He also loved to be a fan and make circles with his hands. His eyes lit up, and he smiled. I really loved when he did this. He looked so happy, and that was a rare experience.

The Door Opens

One day, I decided to sit down with him and make circles with my hands. I told him I was a fan. HE ACTUALLY LOOKED AT ME. It was then I realized, if I entered his world, I could have a relationship with Joe. It was not just accepting him but actually stepping into his world and doing what he was doing. In this way, I got his attention. It was a valuable lesson.

School Issues
Life with Joe was fine until Joe started school and we needed to deal with the outside world. His kindergarten and elementary years were more of a nightmare than anything else. Teachers just did not understand him. Joe had a difficult time in school. He marched to a different drummer and lived in his own world. He paid little, if any, attention to what others were saying to him. Fortunately, middle school and high school were better. Joe seemed to pay better attention to the teachers, who were less traditional in their daily requirements of Joe.

For most of his school years, he sat in the classroom - literally, sat. Just to be there. The teachers sent all of his schoolwork home, where I taught him the concepts. I would get his attention by discussing every concept based on his interests, which at the time were geography and maps. I explained every concept in terms of a map. Actually, that worked and worked well.

Joe was brilliant. Unfortunately, no one knew it but me. Joe not only passed all of his tests to complete elementary and high school but he also went to college. Today, he has a master's degree in political science. Through our experience, I learned to never give up on anyone.

Believe in Our Children
Give kids who struggle a chance. They may surprise you and

achieve far beyond what the professionals expect. I thought Joe was a genius and treated him as if he was a genius. He proved me right. At the time, I did not realize it but I was using a theory called The Looking Glass theory, which said that children picked up on feelings and behaviors of others about them. So, if we believe our children are wonderful, smart, and good, our children will reflect those feelings and internalize them into their own beliefs about themselves. That sets children off in life with a good start; it helps develop self-confidence, self-worth, and self-respect, which is important for any child but especially for a child with special needs.

Being Joe's Mom

Being Joe's mother has been an adventure. It certainly was not the adventure I expected when he was born. It may not be an ideal adventure for anyone else. However, this adventure actually has been perfect for me. It was, however, not so perfect for his father who rarely showed up for parent-teacher meetings and refused to accept Joe having difficulty in school. This is not to say that Joe's father did not love him. It was just that his father could not accept Joe's differences and stopped trying to have any kind of relationship with his son.

Joe did not speak of it, but I could see sadness in his eyes and developing into fear when he became afraid of his father's angry outbursts. That is what finally caused me to seek a divorce. I could not bear the fear in my son's eyes. After years of increasing tensions, the marriage fell apart. To this day, some family members will not accept the fact that Joe is autistic and don't understand what happened with Joe's father. Some still blame me for his father's drinking and abusive behavior. It hurts so but

I continue to do what I believe is best for Joe and me. I am lucky, too, that I have understanding friends who support me.

John Appears

Many years after the divorce, I met a wonderful, loving, understanding man who wanted to marry me, Joe and all. I couldn't believe it. Someone actually wanted to be a part of our little, different family. I told him I would say yes under one condition - that he realize that Joe is my all-important #1. I gave him an out by describing this scenario: If there was one sandwich left in the world, it would go to Joe, and we would watch him eat it and be happy for him. If this man agreed to that, I would marry him. If he didn't, well, we still could be friends. Happily, he agreed. He still agrees 30+ years later. He talks with Joe, interacts with Joe, and enters Joe's world almost as often as I do. Joe has a father. Yes, being the mother of an autistic child changed my life, and it is the best thing that has ever happened to me.

Chapter 5

Theories That Changed My Life

Eric Erikson   Jean Piaget

Out of the Fog

One warm September evening in 1974, I walked into a classroom and listened to the teacher discuss two human development theories that literally changed my life. That evening, in that classroom, the confusion about autism and my son that swirled inside my head began to diminish. Life in terms of human development began to make sense to me. I began to understand my son and his behavior better.

The Autism Puzzle Clears

I began to understand life stage goals to help my son achieve so that he could be more successful in school and later in life. I began putting the pieces of the autism behavior puzzle together. Understanding these theories helped me to put my son's behavior in the context of human development and enabled me to discuss his behavior in more constructive ways with his teachers. Learning these theories made all the difference in the world to me and how I parented my son.

Adapting Theories to Autism

In this book, I present my adapted versions of these developmental theories to reflect how the theories relate to autism. It is my belief that to truly assist an autistic or other special needs child or adult to function well in school, and ultimately in society, one needs to be aware of normal human developmental stages and processes.

Most Helpful to Me

The theories of *Eric Erikson* and *Jean Piaget* are two of my favorite human development theories because they made the most impact on understanding my son. From the first moment I read these theories in my very first college psychology course, I was in awe of the possibilities that they presented for truly understanding our children as they grow and develop. Just as important, or maybe more important, these theories help us to understand the developmental delays experienced by children with certain special needs such as autism.

The Focus

These theories enable us to focus on the important aspects of each stage of childhood and adult development, enabling us to create activities and environments that will assist our in reaching their the desired potential at each stage. These theories helped me focus on the types of activities to include when developing educational and therapeutic programs for the children and adults with whom I have worked.

In Practice

In explaining theory goals to adults in my groups at the clinic, I noticed that my clients were able to better understand themselves and set up their own environments and activities to heal the wounds that caused their problems in the first place.

The Theories

Here, I present these two theories in brief. I also present the social psychology theory of *Charles Cooley*, which provides insight into the infant and childhood sense of self-esteem and self-worth. Other theories included here are the motivational concepts of *Abraham Maslow* and *Albert Bandura* because they help explain the need of children as well as adults to counter dysfunction in their lives. Albert Bandura also is known for his theory on *Social Learning* or *Observational Learning*. This theory helps to understand the impact of adult behavior on the learning process of children.

Eric Erikson's Psychosocial Development Theory

The first theory is that of Eric Erikson's *psychosocial theory of human development* which states that humans develop best and to their potential in the context of social involvement. Each stage of human development involves interaction with others. According to Erikson, each developmental stage has a positive and a negative aspect of development to consider as children grow into adults. Erikson believed it was imperative to know both the positive and the negative aspects of each developmental stage as humans experience both in growing to adulthood. This is important especially if those children have special needs such as autism.

ANATOMY OF ERIKSON'S PSYCHOSOCIAL THEORY
1. Trust vs. Mistrust Infancy: Birth-1 ½
2. Autonomy vs. Shame Early Childhood: 1 ½-3

3. Initiative vs. Guilt Preschool: 3-5
4. Industry vs. Inferiority School age: 5-12
5. Ego Identity vs. Role Confusion Adolescence: 12-18
6. Intimacy vs. Isolation Young Adult: 18-40
7. Generativity vs. Stagnation Adulthood: 40-65
8. Ego Integrity vs. Despair Maturity: 65+

INFANCY: BIRTH TO 18 MONTHS OLD
Trust vs. Mistrust
• According to Erikson, during the first year and a half of life, the major emphasis is on the development of trust.
• Infants learn to trust the caregivers in their lives with their survival. The infant puts out a call and the caregivers respond by satisfying the infant's needs. In this way, the infant feels secure and begins to develop an attachment with the caregivers.
• The important aspect of this stage is the response of caregivers, parents, and other family members to the needs of the infants.
• If the needs of infants are hampered in some way by caregivers not responding satisfactorily to the needs of the infant, mistrust will develop and will negatively affect the second stage of development.
• Unfortunately, this sense of mistrust can follow individuals throughout their lifetime. Trusting that there are others that can and will help in times of need is imperative to developing the ability to explore and take risks in life.
• This sense of trust and secure attachment allows the infant to progress to the second stage with the knowledge that his/her needs will be met, someone will assist if trouble occurs.

TODDLER/EARLY CHILDHOOD YEARS: 18 MONTHS TO 3 YEARS
Autonomy vs. Shame

- In this stage, the toddler becomes an expert in exploration.
- Toddlers need to explore their environment in order to develop a sense of trust in themselves.
- They need to know their physical capabilities.
- If they have developed a sense of trust that their parents or caregivers will save them from frightening situations, they feel free and confident to explore their environment. They will run, climb, and investigate areas like cabinets and closets. In other words, they will get into everything, a necessary stage of development.
- If toddlers do not develop a sense of trust in their caregivers' ability to help them in tough situations, their exploration activities will be dramatically reduced. This will cause a lack of development of skills and knowledge of what they can and will learn to do.
- Instead of developing a sense of autonomy, they become ashamed of their inability to develop skills. This can lead to a sense of inferiority and lack of motivation later in life.

PRESCHOOLER: 3 TO 5 YEARS
Initiative vs. Guilt
- During this stage, children learn to try out their newfound skills by engaging in creative activities. They want to do things.
- Their play changes from parallel play (playing in the same way near to each other) to interactive play (actually interacting with each other during play). Now, they truly want to interact with others. They will initiate play with parents and other family members and friends.
- Being able to attend preschool and socialize helps with the development of initiative. Children at this stage observe adults in

their environment and mimic their behavior in specialized ways. Girls will observe their mothers and other women in their environment and mimic their behaviors. The boys do the same with their fathers and other men.

- In this stage, initiating activities and projects is important. This sense of initiation prepares them for the next stage of becoming industrious. If it is hampered, children can feel a sense of guilt because they have a strong desire to engage with others. Even though they are denied the interaction or told "no," the sense of having "bad" desires and feeling guilt can be carried into adulthood.

SCHOOL AGE CHILD: 6 TO 12 YEARS
Industry vs. Inferiority
- During this stage, children develop a sense of industry and competence.
- This not only is a skill-building stage, but it also is a stage of successful completion. The pleasure that children feel in successfully completing a project enables them to develop the motivation to begin and complete the next project or goal.
- It is up to parents and teachers to know the skill level and learning capability of children so they can properly develop activities, projects, and goals that lead children to experience successful completion. This means parents and teachers need to know the children as they are, not as they want them to be.
- If children do not experience successful completion of goals and projects, the pleasure of success and therefore the sense of motivation is not properly developed. The children grow up feeling inferior to others their age.
- They lack a sense of motivation for completing goals because

they do not believe that they can achieve the goals. They believe that they lack skills to achieve goals successfully. They also can believe that they lack the ability to learn skills well enough to complete activities successfully.
• Unfortunately, lack of self-confidence can be a lifelong problem causing motivation problems in every aspect of life.

ADOLESCENT: 12 TO 18 YEARS
Identity vs. Role Confusion
• In this stage, adolescents struggle to discover their own identity: who they are, what they can and cannot do, and their eventual place in society.
• They are on the threshold of adulthood and need to make decisions and commitments. They need to evaluate themselves not only with respect to their abilities and skills but also with respect to their likes and dislikes, interests, values, and sense of morality.
• The search to know themselves is quite a task, and some do not sufficiently complete this stage. Some will give up and accept how they are defined by others such as parents or friends.
• These adolescents become confused about who they are and run the risk of not growing into satisfying adult roles.
• These adolescents become confused about who they are and run the risk of not growing into satisfying adult roles.
• Our role in society as an adult depends on our personal investigation and realistic evaluation of who we are and our place in society.

YOUNG ADULT: 18 TO 40 YEARS
Intimacy vs. Isolation
• At this young adult stage, the focus is on developing more

mature long-term relationships and making long-term commitments.
- It is in this stage that parents and educators realize the importance of positive development during the previous stages.
- Young adults socialize not only for mere interaction but also for the development of long-lasting relationships, including the possibility of finding marriage partners.
- In order to offer oneself in friendship or love, one must first know oneself. This is why positive development in the prior stages is so important.
- Self-identity is vital before one can develop true, meaningful relationships.
- As young adults progress through this stage, they acquire social skills that lead to intimate relationships.
- If a young adult has difficulty socializing and developing intimate relationships, they run the risk of feeling isolated, which can lead to sadness, loneliness, and depression.

MIDDLE-AGED ADULT: 35 OR 40 TO 65
Generativity vs. Stagnation
- Career and an interest in helping others/making a difference are the important aspects of this stage.
- Middle-aged adults can take on greater responsibilities as they couple career with creating a family.
- They make their way in society and find satisfying roles that allow them to feel they are making a positive difference in the world.
- This stage can lead to the culmination of life goals such as reaching desired success in a career or watching children

grow and develop into happy, healthy adults.
- Major changes in life, like job shifts or "empty nest syndrome," can cause a reevaluation of life goals and desires.
- This is a stage that focuses on being a positive, contributing member of society through work and/or by raising a family. Either way, the middle-aged adult is contributing to the benefit of society.
- If, however, an individual progresses through these stages in a negative manner, they are unable to achieve a sense of positively contributing to society. Instead, they develop a lack of self-esteem and self-worth.
- Dissatisfaction with life, including relationships and career, are common with negative development in this stage.

LATE ADULT: 65 TO DEATH
Integrity vs. Despair
- In this last stage of Erikson's human development, the mature adult ideally develops a sense of integrity. This sense of integrity depends, of course, on the positive development of previous stages.
- In this stage, the individual looks back on his or her life and acknowledges the positive and negative aspects of their life.
- It is important to realistically evaluate what has been accomplished and what was left undone. It is a time to find value in life situations and understand that lessons were learned even when mistakes were made.
- It also is a time to pass this wisdom to the next generation. Usually, elderly adults pass accrued knowledge onto their grandchildren, which is ideal. The elderly need to reminisce, and adolescent grandchildren need to find their identity. These two generations help each other to accomplish a life stage goal.

- If elderly adults do not find value in what they have accomplished, despair may set in along with severe depression. At this stage, the older individual may need assistance in finding value in their lives. Being too self-critical can impede the development of integrity or self-worth. Familiar people can step in and help them take stock of their life accomplishments.

JEAN PIAGET'S COGNITIVE DEVELOPMENT THEORY

The second theory that I find valuable in helping to understand an autistic child/adult is the cognitive developmental theory of Jean Piaget. This theory has only four stages but packs enough information into those four stages to enable us to understand cognitive development from infancy through adulthood. Piaget helps us to understand the differences between the thought processes and reasoning abilities of adults and children by demonstrating how children begin to learn adult reasoning.

Jean Piaget created a theory of cognitive development because he believed that children learned and reasoned differently than adults. Th rough observing his own children, he became aware of a developmental process in which children learned to think and reason.

Piaget is an organic theorist, meaning that he believed that when the brain was ready to learn, the child would be motivated to actively set out to learn. He developed four stages of cognitive development that allow us to better understand how a child thinks and why they think differently than adults.

Anatomy of Cognitive Development
1. Sensory Motor: Birth to 2 years.
2. Preoperational Thinking: Ages 2-6
3. Concrete Operational Thinking: Ages 7-12

4. Formal Operational Thinking: Ages 12-Adult

SENSORIMOTOR STAGE (BIRTH TO 2 YEARS OLD) AWARENESS OF ENVIRONMENT
• The first stage of cognitive development focuses on how the infant becomes aware of the environment.
• Infants obtain information through the five senses.
• It stresses the necessity of the infant to move the body so the acquired information "gels" in the brain.
• Creating a safe environment for the infant is required for positive cognitive development.

PREOPERATIONAL STAGE (AGES 2 TO 6)
SYMBOLISM, LANGUAGE DEVELOPMENT, IMAGINATION
• The second stage of cognitive development is one of symbolism, fantasy, imagination, and language development.
• Language is a code of both verbal and written symbols.
• It is the ideal stage for learning a language, or two or three!
• This stage focuses on the imagination of the child.
• Stories in books are truly alive for the child who can, at times, confuse the fantasy of the story with the reality of life, making life with a child of this age very interesting.
• A child at this stage can only conceptualize one aspect of an item or situation at a time. For example, a glass is short or tall, wide or slender.
• The child at this age is incapable of understanding the idea that something short and wide or tall and slender can hold the same amount of water.
• The children at this stage have no concept of sharing. Children understand the world in their own terms, only from their own perspective. Therefore, if they want to play with a particular toy,

they believe everyone would like them to have and play with the toy. The children at this age are confused when another child wants to play with the same toy they want. Sharing is a difficult concept for children at this age. It must be taught with patience and tolerance.

CONCRETE OPERATIONAL THINKING (AGES 7 TO 12)
AGE OF REASON
- In this third stage of cognitive development, the child becomes a true thinking being.
- Before this stage, Piaget believed children did not have the ability to reason or think rationally, hence, seven was considered the age of reason.
- In this stage, children need to DO things in order to learn. Reading and writing are good activities, but developing projects, going on field trips, and doing experiments are necessary for true learning to take place.
- In this stage, children learn to classify and serialize objects (i.e. put them in logical order).
- It is a time when many children develop collections.
- Problem-solving is accomplished through trial-and-error. Each solution must be either discussed or actively tried in order to understand if it would actually solve the problem.
- Piaget believed humans are active learners and required performing activities in order to commit acquired information to memory or to truly understand concepts.
- The focus is on concrete or hands-on aspects of thinking and learning.

FORMAL OPERATIONAL THINKING (AGES 12 TO Adult)
ABSTRACT THINKING
- The fourth and last stage of cognitive development is the attainment of abstract thinking.
- This stage begins around age 12 and "gels" at about 25. However, abstract thinking continues to develop well into late adulthood.
- In this stage, one can "see" into the future to evaluate consequences of present behavior. In previous stages, one was not capable of doing that and needed to be told of the consequences of behavior, decisions that had taken place.
- In abstract thinking, the adult can problem-solve by projecting solutions into the future to evaluate the outcome. The adult can then decide if the outcome is to their liking even before any action is taken.
- This is a tenuous cognitive stage, however. If the adult is sick, stressed, anxious, or traumatized, he/she reverts to the previous stage of concrete thinking. This may be why some professionals believe autistic adults do not develop abstract thinking. Autistic adults usually experience great anxiety and often revert back to concrete thinking processes.

Not Really a Flaw

Erikson's and Piaget's theories are highly respected, but they do not make allowances for special needs children and adults. Since these theories were written in the early twentieth century, this omission is not a flaw but is due to the lack of knowledge about autism at the time. My adaptations of Erikson's and Piaget's theories designed to assist parents and teachers of autistic individuals are presented in the chapters of Section Two.

CHARLES H. COOLEY: THE LOOKING GLASS THEORY

Charles Cooley's theory provides insight into the development of some of the emotional problems experienced by children with differences or special needs. This theory helps increase the awareness of subtle expressions that can negatively affect children as young as infants. We might be able to monitor our verbal expressions directed to children, but we usually have extreme difficulty monitoring our facial expressions. Even when we quickly change our facial expressions, children as young as toddlers can identify negative expressions related to them.

Highlights of This Theory Are:
• This social psychology theory explains how children learn their own worth and value through the positive or negative reactions of their parents, caregivers, and others.
• Infants can pick up subtle inferences of likes or dislikes in parents' facial expressions, voices, and body language. They develop a concept of how an adult feels about them.
• Remember, the infant looks to parents and caregivers as objects for survival so parents and caregivers are all-important. If it seems like the parent does not like the infant or child, the infant interprets it as something wrong with him/herself, not the parent.
• The infant then accepts this interpretation of him/herself as real and reflects that belief in subsequent behavior.
• In this theory, facial expressions and behaviors of a parent or caregiver act like a mirror to the infant so that the infant picks up the attitude and beliefs about him/herself as true.
• This can be good for an infant who is loved by those around him/her. However, it can be very destructive when doubt or

displeasure are relayed to the infant. This happens quite often with infants who are disabled in some way and do not act like the anticipated "normal" infant.
- Infants mirror what their parents think of them for good or bad. We must try to be as loving to them in our words, expressions, and actions as possible.

MOTIVATION THEORIES

Here are two theories on motivation by Abraham Maslow and Albert Bandura, respectively. Motivation is an important concept because it spurs us on and fires us up to initiate and persist in completing goals successfully, no matter how difficult.

Motivation is the result of accomplishing goals in childhood and experiencing the pleasure of successfully achieving those goals.

ABRAHAM MASLOW:
THEORY OF MOTIVATION BASED ON NEEDS

Maslow presents a hierarchy of needs that each human must achieve to actualize their own personal potential. As we achieve or satisfy each need, the next one emerges. Humans are motivated to satisfy each need in the hierarchy. Maslow was a humanistic theorist who believed that each person is born with a core of potential, and it is that individual's life task to achieve or actualize that potential. It is a theory that helps psychologists, school psychologists included, to identify what is missing for children and adults experiencing dysfunction in their lives.

Anatomy of Maslow's Hierarchy of Needs
1. Physiological Needs: Food, drink, sleep
2. Safety Needs: Safe in one's environment
3. Love and Belonging Needs: Belonging to a group

4. Self-Esteem Needs: Self-worth/respect, others' respect
5. Self-Actualization: Actualizing/achieving one's potential

Physiological Needs
• Satisfying physiological needs is the starting point for Maslow's theory of motivation.
• It is important to maintain a constant state of balance.
• Cravings are preferential choices among foods and indicates what is needed.
• If the body lacks a vitamin or mineral, the individual will tend to develop a specific hunger or craving for that food.

Safety Needs
• Infants, children, and adults react to safety needs.
• Each age group displays different behaviors when feeling threatened.
• Children, including autistic children and adults prefer a safe, orderly, predictable, and organized world.
• A peaceful society usually makes its members feel safe.
• Safety reflects a preference for the familiar rather than the unfamiliar.

Love and Belonging Needs
• Love and affection, regardless of the source, provide a sense of belonging to the developing child as well as the adult.

Esteem Needs
• Desire for a stable positive evaluation of our selves by others results in a sense of self-respect and high self-esteem.
• Esteem is based upon actual capabilities, achievement, and respect from others.
• There is a desire for strength, achievement, adequacy,

confidence, independence, and freedom as well as reputation, recognition, attention, and appreciation.
- Achieving these needs leads to feelings of self-confidence, worth, strength, capability, and adequacy along with a sense of being useful and necessary in the world.
- Thwarting these needs leads to feelings of inferiority, weakness, and helplessness, discouragement, and neuroticism.

Self-Actualization
- This involves the desire for self-fulfillment or reaching our potential. We need to realistically evaluate our abilities and interests to create a life and career plan that reflects who we are and how we function in society.

ALBERT BANDURA:
MOTIVATION BASED ON SELF-ESTEEM

Albert Bandura explains particularly well the importance of achieving self-esteem. He focuses on an individual's abilities and skills. Self-esteem and self-worth are important considerations for all human beings, including autistic children and adults.

Albert Bandura: Achievement of Self-Esteem
- **Self-Efficacy:** The belief that we can behave in a manner that produces successful outcomes.
- **Efficacy Expectations**: Convictions that one can successfully execute the behavior required to produce the desired outcomes.
- **Efficacy Outcomes**: Estimates that a given behavior will lead to certain outcomes.

Persona Mastery
Expectations of personal mastery affect both the initiation and persistence of coping behavior. The strength of people's

convictions in their own effectiveness affects whether they will try to cope with given situations.

Bandura's Social Learning Theory
Bandura also is noted for his *Social Learning Theory*, which helps parents and teachers understand the learning process that takes place when a child is observing others in their environment.

This theory includes the following concepts:
- **Role models**: the idea that children readily imitate behavior exhibited by a model in the presence of the model.
- **Observational Learning**: the process by which children observe adults and other children and learn the observed behavior, whether positive or negative. Focuses on learning behavior solely through the process of observation. No instruction needs to take place. Learning is saved for future use.

Motivation Based on Perceived Rewards
When the child or adult is motivated, observed behavior will be performed. Vicarious learning occurs when children and adults are motivated to perform a behavior based on whether they will be rewarded for that behavior. The reward can be an actual, concrete reward such as candy or praise, or it can be the belief that the behavior will be enjoyed.

Motivation based on Perceived Internal Rewards
Children and adults observe whether another individual(s) is enjoying certain behavior. If so, the child or adult is more likely to perform the behavior at some point in the future. If the child or adult observes pain or dissatisfaction, the child or adult is less likely to perform that behavior in the future.

Avoiding Punishment

If the observed behavior is enjoyed but is punished by someone in authority, the child or adult takes this aspect into consideration. Sense of enjoyment is a powerful attraction and highly motivating. The child or adult will be motivated to try the behavior but what is learned is that the behavior is punishable. The child or adult is careful not to perform the behavior in the presence of an authority figure who can administer punishment. The child or adult has not learned to avoid performing the punishable behavior; they learn to avoid performing it in the presence of an authority figure.

Section Two

Developmental Life Spans As They Relate to Autism: Life with Joe

Chapter 6

Joe Finally Sleeps

Infancy

The Incredible First Year

The first year of a child's life is absolutely fascinating. Infants start out as cute little "baby dolls" who eat, cry, and dirty diapers. Then, right before our eyes, they miraculously develop into little persons with a true personality, communication skills, and a desire to investigate the exciting world surrounding them.

Insights on Infancy

Infancy is birth and 1 to 1 ½ years of age. Because infants can't take care of themselves, they rely on parents, their primary caregivers. This is the stage when trust between parents and infants develop. As we care for our infants, they develop trust believing they can count on us to always be there to take care of them. This trust is vital in developing a true relationship with our infant children.

Infancy is also a prime time for learning as infants are sponges using their senses to soak up information about their environment. Whether we realize it or not, infants are taking in everything, seeing, hearing, smelling, touching, and can feel stress, even the stress of others.

Some very telling characteristics of autism show up as early as infancy, such as they may not want to be held closely or may not sleep well. They usually have ear infections and high fevers at a statistically higher rate. The cause of these characteristics is still unknown. What it means, however, is that the experiences of parents of autistic infants are different, sometimes very different, than those of parents of non-autistic infants.

Life with Joe: Achieving Trust

Eight days after Joe was born, we were able to leave the hospital. His grandparents waited for us at home, barely able to contain their excitement to see him, hold him, and cuddle him. It was a hot, sunny day in mid-July. Everything seemed normal until late that night. Joe wouldn't fall asleep. When I picked him up and held him closely, he cried louder. I tried to feed him and change his diaper, but nothing seemed to comfort him. Finally, I propped a pillow under my arm for support and held him on my lap for hours. He fell asleep.

The Signs Were There

In Joe's first year, the signs of autism were there clear as a bell. No one, especially me, knew what all the problems Joe experienced meant. Joe's birth was difficult, and both Joe and I were lucky to come out of it alive. He had ear infections and high fevers. He had a fatty tumor in his stomach causing eating problems. He had difficulty falling asleep at night and seemed sensitive to touch and sounds. In today's world all of these scream AUTISM. But NOT in 1966.

From the very beginning of his life, Joe was different. He did not seem to connect with people and was happy in his own world. I could not have any other children so I wanted to make the most of Joe's infancy. I wanted to hold and cuddle him but he always squirmed and cried. Of course, I thought this not wanting to be held or cuddled on Joe's part was due to something that I might have done. I never once considered the problem to be him. I was the parent, I was the adult. What was I doing wrong to cause my baby to not want to be held and cuddled? I knew babies needed to count on or trust someone to help them with whatever they needed. So, I tried to resolve each of these problems doing anything and everything I could think of doing. I set up an hourly schedule to feed him small amounts of formula so as to not overwhelm his little stomach and never have him really be hungry. He must have internalized the schedule and trusted that the next meal was coming soon. After several months, the tumor disappeared. Then, feeding was a different story. Joe wanted to eat - and eat, he did. He drank his formula, not quite guzzling but faster than ever before. He ate his baby vegetables and fruit with a smile on his face, trying to grab the spoon to lick every morsel. He ate with gusto and pleasure for the first time in his life.

The Nightmare of Sleep

If eating had initially been a problem, sleeping was a nightmare. No pun intended. Joe did not like to go to bed. He was born at two minutes after midnight, and he considered the middle of the night as play time. This has been a lifelong sleep pattern but was especially a nightmare during the school years.

I would put Joe to bed at a decent hour - around eight or nine o'clock in the evening. Joe did not go for it. He would cry until his little face was red and wet with tears. One night as he was jumping up and down in his crib, the crib's springs broke. He was holding on the bars and screaming. It was pure luck that he had not fallen to the floor and hurt himself. After that incident, I no longer wanted to put him to bed so early. It never worked. Joe was miserable; therefore, I was miserable. Why continue?

An Idea
I had an idea that I thought might work to calm Joe at bedtime. Joe had an infant swing that he loved during the day so I thought that I would give it a try at bedtime. He loved it. He would swing all evening and fall asleep a little after midnight. I would then carefully pick him up and put him in his crib. No luck. Each time, he would wake up. He would not sleep through my carrying him to the crib. He would cry when he found himself in his crib. I was finally getting the hint that Joe did not like his crib. Not sure of what to do, I would put him back in the swing and start all over.

Another Idea
Then, another thought: Why not try to calm him in the crib instead of putting him back in the swing? When he woke in the crib, I would lightly stroke his cheek and forehead to soothe him. It worked beautifully. Joe would calm down and begin to fall asleep. If I stopped stroking his cheek, he would wake up and cry in displeasure, so I soothed him for hours. Most nights, I fell

asleep hanging over the crib's bars. Joe was sleeping comfortably in his crib while I was sleeping uncomfortably hanging half upside down. Well, he was happy. And if he was happy, I was happy. It was a little unconventional, but it worked for us.

Yes, I knew something was wrong when it came to Joe sleeping in his crib. I just did not know what was wrong nor what to do. All I knew was that something upset him there. He seemed okay if I was stroking his cheek. He seemed to relax and fall asleep. At about 4 a.m., I was able to go to bed without waking Joe. And gratefully, he would sleep until 9 or 10 a.m. He did get enough sleep. It was just at different times than most other infants.

That Lonely Feeling

When Joe was almost a year old, I started to put stuffed animals in his crib with him. He seemed to like that. I had hesitated to do so earlier because I thought t he might suffocate. Now, he could move and turn over. He had more control of his body movements. I thought I would give it a try because maybe Joe was lonely in his crib. He had a favorite animal that he held during the day, a small, fluffy dog. It was small enough for him to carry, and it was soft. I think he liked the softness near his skin.

I put the stuffed animal beside Joe, he took it from my hand and held it. Holding the stuffed animal helped him go to sleep faster. I still needed to soothe him, but not for so long into the night. Joe was not alone in the crib any longer.

No Lockdown

Later on, I noticed Joe was calm and happy in his crib with his stuffed animal but became anxious when I put up the crib bars. I had never noticed that before. The bars were for his safety, so I kept them up and soothed him until he fell asleep. One night, however, I decided to keep the bars down. I was nervous. What if he climbed out and hurt himself in the middle of the night? Seeing the anxious look on his face made me give it a try. The bars were down, Joe picked up his stuffed animal and held it. He started to fall asleep. I was shocked. He already had been in the swing and then I read him a story as usual. The only difference was the bars. I wondered if that had been the problem all along. Once I kept the bars down, he did not need me to soothe him. After a while, he did not need the swing any longer. He could go to bed about 10 p.m. or so and would lie there touching his beloved stuffed animals and treasured books. When he was ready, he would fall asleep. Joe learned to trust that if he was experiencing a problem, I would pay attention to the subtle changes on his face and try to help. I think he learned that we were a team able to resolve problems, even if it did take some time. I was successfully becoming a detective, a real-life Agatha Christie's Miss Marple.

Being Comfortable/Ready to Learn

Solving problems and helping Joe be more comfortable in his surroundings, no matter what those surroundings happened to be, enabled him to be more relaxed and ready to learn. Babies learn by absorbing information through their five senses. Even though autistic babies have sensory sensitivity, they still learn through their senses. Parents just need to develop an environment that is less sensory stressful, so our autistic babies learn and develop just like other babies.

We need to expose our autistic infants to as many interesting, colorful objects as possible, allowing them to examine everything they can. Babies touch, smell, and taste everything within reach. Of course, parents find this need to touch and taste everything frustrating. However, it's necessary for basic learning babies require. I believed it was important for Joe to explore the house just as all other babies do but so many things around the house bothered him and caused him to retreat, close down. I didn't want my baby to just sit there doing nothing. I wanted him to be active, exploring and loving every minute of it.

So, to accomplish this, I really went against the grain of common thought. Most parents at the time kept their homes as they were before their infants could move around. My friends and family insisted that, like other babies, Joe needed to learn to obey when told, "No." I, on the other hand, went against that philosophy. I took away everything that could break and harm Joe. I replaced them with colorful plastic and wooden blocks and toys. I wanted Joe to move around and play. I wanted him to reach out and touch safe objects that would teach him something. It seemed like common sense to me. I got a lot of grief from family and friends for this but I wanted Joe to explore. I wanted him to touch objects and examine them. I wanted him to taste most everything he touched. After "redecorating" the house, Joe explored everything and seemed like he was having fun. I was having fun watching him have fun. I said "no" to him touching outlets and the stove enough times during the day that he did learn what "no" meant. I didn't know, then, that allowing Joe to touch and taste things was important at this stage of his life. I was just having fun watching him play.

Learning: A Happening Thing
Like many children, Joe had blocks with letters on them, and each

letter was a different color. Every time he picked up a block, I would say the letter and the color of the letter. By two years old, he actually was learning the alphabet quite easily. He loved his letters and colors. He loved his books and wanted a story every night. I put colorful toys on tables and windowsills to encourage him to get up and reach for things. He liked to watch television sometimes but really liked to wander around.

Noticing Differences

Joe was a sponge. He was learning so many things, but in that first year, I already noticed he was different from other babies. I had been with my nephew, Nick (who was 16 months older than Joe), for most of the year before Joe was born and had observed him and his style of interacting with others. Joe was so different. At first, I just thought it was Joe. He had a different personality than Nick. Joe seemed to learn so easily but when it came to verbal communication, there was a real difference between the two. My nephew spoke to and interacted with others easily. He loved to be with other children and made eye contact when speaking. Joe, on the other hand, rarely spoke to or interacted with others. He rarely made eye contact. I noticed it, accepted it, and went on doing what I needed to do for Joe. Even if Joe did not verbally interact with people in the way most children do, he had a lot of sensory and motor experiences that first year. He observed and explored his environment and seemed to enjoy learning. He would point to objects and wait for me to name them. After he heard the words several times, he would move on to another item or object in the house. He was eager to learn. I knew from the very beginning that Joe was intelligent and learning came easily to him.

Such a Good Baby
In his first year, Joe was physically uncomfortable due to high fevers and earaches. He had a strange sleep schedule, to say the least. Given all of that, he actually was a good baby. When he was not in pain or discomfort, he would smile. He looked so beautiful when he smiled. He smiled when trying to reach his colorful mobile in his crib. He smiled when I held our parakeet up to him. He smiled when I held him in the air as if he was flying. He smiled when he held his fluffy stuffed dog.

I would sing to Joe while I fed him, changed his diaper, and bathed him. I would tell him how beautiful he was and usually sing that to him as well. I would tell him that he was my beauty and my angel. I still tell him that today. I can't help myself. I wanted Joe to feel loved even though he didn't like being hugged or cuddled. I truly believe Joe knew that I loved him.

Oh, But Others
His father, however, was a different story. Joe's father had very little interaction with Joe after the first two weeks of Joe's birth, and Joe and his father rarely played together. Joe's father never read to him at night nor tried to comfort him when going to sleep. I don't think it was that his father didn't love Joe. I think that Joe's father just did not know what to do with a baby and had difficulty learning to be a dad. Joe's father was embarrassed that his son was different from other infants. Differences may have been easier to tolerate from a distance. And Joe's father kept his distance.

My parents and Joe's paternal grandparents loved him and expressed it. However, his paternal grandmother was somewhat uncomfortable with Joe around other family members especially if she was entertaining. She just would not invite us. She loved Joe very much but could not deal with his different behavior when other family members were present. Joe was an interesting child, to say the least. As long as I could resolve the problematic situations such as his sleeping habits, everything was fine. We then quickly, too quickly, progressed to toddlerhood.

ACHIEVING LIFE STAGE GOALS

The Autistic Difference: Infancy

- *Trust others---Erikson*

Process vs. Components
The process of developing trust for autistic infants is similar to non-autistic infants but the components can be different. A parent/caregiver responds to infant cries by picking up the infant and cuddling him/her. This is the normal response when we believe an infant needs comforting. However, the autistic infant may have an adverse reaction to being held and cuddled. Some autistic infants have sensitive nerve endings in their skin causing uncomfortable or painful feelings when held, cuddled.

Therefore, a parent/caregiver of an autistic infant might need to modify their response to a crying autistic infant since cuddling may cause more intense crying. Instead, a soothing voice will allow the infant to realize that the caregiver is responding and will satisfy his/ her needs.

Tolerance Level
Being aware of the comfort level of the infant will guide parents/caregivers in the level of closeness the infant can tolerate. Some infants can tolerate being held for only short

periods of time while others may be able to tolerate longer periods. Some infants do not fuss when being held close to a parent while others do not want to be cuddled at all. It truly depends on the level of touch the infant can bear.

Awareness

Autistic infants may not cry when they are hungry or have a wet diaper because they are not aware of the discomfort of being hungry or wet. Consequently, monitoring the feeding schedule and diaper change times is important for caregivers of an autistic infant. Keeping a schedule of the times and amounts of food is important to predict when an autistic infant might be hungry or need a diaper change. Just because an autistic infant is unaware of the discomfort does not mean the infant is immune to the consequences of the discomfort. He/she will still have a drop in blood sugar when hungry or develop a rash from sitting in a wet diaper too long. A monitoring schedule is important.

Developing Attachment

Autistic infants may not make eye contact or smile at parents. These are important behaviors in developing trust and especially attachment. Parents/caregivers of autistic infants may feel the infant is dismissing them or does not like them. It is necessary for parents to realize that these feelings are not the reality of the situation. The infant needs the parent and depends on the parent. The autistic infant just expresses this need differently from what parents expect, but the objective at this stage is still to build trust. Parents of autistic infants must continue to smile at the infant, speak to the infant, and respond to the infant's cries, satisfying their needs. In this way, parents help autistic infants to develop trust that they will always be there for them.

Self-Soothing Techniques

Allow for infant self-soothing: suck his/her thumb or suck on a corner of a blanket. Self-soothing in autistic infants and children is especially imperative due to the problems they have in recognizing their needs and asking for the assistance in satisfying these needs.

As autistic infants grow, the self-soothing becomes automatic and allows them to reduce the discomfort they feel but cannot verbalize. Rocking is a hallmark of autism and soothes the child.

The Autistic Difference: *Infancy*

- *Obtain information through the senses, importance of movement---Piaget*

Attention Level

The first step in cognitive development for autistic infants is to gauge their level of response to items and events in their environment. Some autistic infants will attend to people and items in the environment easily while other autistic infants will need motivation to attend to any or every person or item in the environment. Even though the infant may not respond to items and events in his/her environment in the same way as a non-autistic infant, the infant is still acquiring information through his/her senses.

Setting Up the Environment

Parents/caregivers need to set up the environment to enhance the motivation of the autistic infant to observe and take in information. An important environmental element for infants, especially autistic infants, is opportunities for activity. Activities such as presenting the infant with items of different colors and varying types of sounds (not too loud) help caregivers to understand which colors and sounds the infant will observe for longer periods of time. Presenting various colors and sounds not only helps keep an infant interested in interacting with the environment but also helps the infant begin to notice similarities and differences in objects and sounds, which is a key element in the learning process.

Learning

Absorbing information is not the only process important to learning: grouping similar objects, classifying objects, and recognizing why an object does not belong to a particular group are vital elements to the later learning process. The longer caregivers can engage their child, the better. Longer periods of engagement result in longer periods of learning.

It is beneficial to talk or sing to all infants since this helps to develop the foundation for language structure. Talking and singing to autistic infants accomplishes the same thing. The tone of voice, level of pitch, and degree of volume will affect the autistic infant in different ways than these variations would affect a non-autistic infant.

Sounds

Sounds with certain pitches or tones (particularly high ones such as whistles and sirens) may be uncomfortable for the autistic infant just as certain types of touch can negatively affect him/her. Many sounds at once may overwhelm an autistic infant, causing him/her to shut down and no longer engage or interact. Observing the reaction and response of an autistic infant is important, as is testing levels of sounds and intensities of color.

We certainly do not want to cause distress to our autistic infants while we are trying to motivate them to interact with people and objects in the environment.

Touch

Because of neurological differences, many autistic infants react negatively to touch, and it is wise to begin touching the infant slowly and lightly. Lightly touching or stroking an infant's cheek, hands, or feet desensitizes the infant to touch, and allows the infant to become more comfortable and more easily tolerate the touching experience. Touching objects helps the infant acquire information, so it is necessary to help him/her not only be comfortable touching objects but also to begin to enjoy touching objects.

Likes and Dislikes

One of the most valuable tasks for a caregiver of an autistic infant is to know their infant's likes and dislikes, including their level of tolerance for sensory experiences in the environment. These activities help parents develop an attachment relationship with their autistic infants while developing trust and stimulating cognitive development. An infant must interact with his/her environment for the brain to develop and the learning process to begin.

Looking Glass: Self-Esteem--Cooley

Infancy is the beginning of self-esteem, self-worth, and self-understanding. How parents, teachers, caregivers feel about the infant reflects on their facial expressions, body language, and tone of voice. Infants can and do pick up on the subtleties of feelings and, in time, internalize the feelings of others as what is true about themselves. When interacting with infants, be mindful of the feelings being expressed even subtly to the infant for those feelings will become part of the infants self-view as he/she grows and develops.

Needs Based Motivation--Maslow
Satisfaction of needs is especially strong in infancy as each of the needs is satisfied by others. Satisfying an infant's needs in a timely manner builds trust between infant and caregiver. However, it also sends a message to the infant that he/she is worth the effort of others. Each need on the hierarchy is vital to the sense of worth and self-esteem of the infant which, in turn, helps motivate the infant to learn and eventually become independent.

Ability Based Motivation--Bandura
Infants learn mainly through the five senses. As infants move, the information gathered through the senses "gels" in the brain developing parts of the brain for future functioning. Encouraging infants to use their senses moving allows the infant to lay a foundation for understanding their abilities motivating them to continue to observe and interact with their environment.

Chapter 7

Joe Explores

 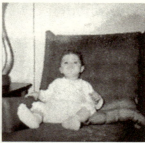

Toddlerhood

The Terrible Twos?
There is a great amount of learning happening in this stage and every day brings new adventures.

Insights on Toddlerhood
Toddlerhood falls in the 1 ½-3 years range and is the stage of significant exploring both their own abilities leading to autonomy and independence and their environment to gather more information about the world around them. Toddlers continue to gather knowledge through their senses but now they are more mobile, their world is wider causing parents to be more vigilant. During toddlerhood, a child begins to develop his or her own personality and temperament. That is not to say that they did not show some personality and temperament as infants, but during toddlerhood, many more of these traits become apparent. You can begin to see the mini-person they may become. They are doing more at this stage, and we, as parents, realize that our children need to begin to develop some sense of independence. They begin to communicate verbally with us. They want to feed themselves. They want to bathe themselves. We hear them say

"ME" often. They want to accomplish tasks by themselves.

Autism and Autonomy

This sense of independence through autonomy can be different in autistic toddlers, who can be nonverbal at this stage and will express this desire in different ways. Parents of autistic toddlers should understand that their toddlers want to be independent and autonomous, but they must observe their toddlers for subtle signs that they are ready for autonomous activities. Autistic toddlers may gesture instead of speaking. They may point to or reach out for desired items. Autistic toddlers can make subtle facial movements to express a desire to perform an activity or examine an object. Staring at objects or closely watching an activity may alert parents to the fact that the autistic toddler is ready to experiment. The key is to observe our autistic toddlers for the subtle signs signaling their readiness to explore.

Life with Joe: Achieving Autonomy

Joe's toddlerhood was one of the happiest and most interesting times of my life. I experienced the wonder of the world through the eyes of a two year old. It was as if I was seeing the world for the first time. Joe and I took walks around our neighborhood and bus rides to see other neighborhoods. Joe was fascinated by signs. The excitement he felt when recognizing a letter or color was infectious. People walking or riding the bus with us smiled at Joe and sometimes said the letters and colors with us. Joe loved exploring whether it was in his room, in our home, on walks, or bus rides.

What can I say about two- and three-year-old toddlers? They are so much fun at this stage, curious and mobile. When you have a toddler in the home, there is never a dull moment. The toddler's curiosity will motivate him/her to explore closets, cabinets, and toilets. Nothing is out of bounds, even if parents disagree. If it is there, it is ready to be explored.

Differences More Prominent

This was the stage of Joe's development when I realized that he was truly different. He was not as verbal as other children, and he was content to be alone instead of interacting with other children or adults. I really did not know what to do about the differences I saw in Joe, from his lack of eye contact to his lack of understanding what was happening around him. I just went along with whatever he was doing. As it turned out, this was the best decision in the long run.

Entering Joe's World

By just being with Joe and doing what he was doing or wanted to do, I learned how to enter his world. The first time was quite by accident. It happened when I sat on the floor next to Joe. He was doing his favorite activity, pretending to be a fan by making circles with his hands. It was a fluke on my part but I decided to be a fan, too. Making circles with my hands caught Joe's attention. He looked at my hands. Then, he looked at me. He looked at ME. He made eye contact and actually saw me AND smiled. For several minutes, we both sat on the dining room floor and pretended to be fans. I could not think of a better place to be. Through my fan experiment, I entered Joe's world. I knew then what it took to become part of his world. I found a way that I could actually play with him and be with him. Entering his world was a practice that I would use over and over as he grew up.

Seeing the World Differently
For the parent of an autistic toddler, this stage can be especially interesting since autistic children perceive the world a little differently than non-autistic children. I was fascinated by Joe's developing personality and experimenting behavior. As he began to walk at eight months old, he seemed motivated to move and explore his environment. He touched everything, and when he could not reach the enticing objects that seemed to call to him, he learned to stand on tiptoes. He actually was very good at solving the problems he encountered in exploring his world. He seemed less distressed when exploring than at any other time.

Encouraging Exploration
Joe was a little bundle of curiosity, learning and gathering information about his environment and about himself. He discovered what he was capable of doing and what he was not capable of doing. The latter did not seem to inhibit him at all. He just kept on trying until he achieved what he set out to do. This is, in fact, very much like any toddler.
However, interacting with people continued to elude him, as Joe did all of these activities alone. It did not matter to him if someone was in the same room or not; he proceeded to do his exploring. He did not include cousins, or children of friends, in his activities. He did it all by himself. I removed as many breakable objects as possible from our home, replacing them with colorful toys such as blocks and balls. He noticed them and in due time

would crawl, walk, reach, and climb to take them and examine them. Touching, looking, tasting, smelling, and shaking were behaviors that happened with just about every object he acquired. Interestingly, he examined these objects and when satisfied with what he had learned about them, he would replace them where he found them. He did not toss them on the floor or throw them away. He very carefully replaced them where he found them. I fleetingly wondered about his "neatness" but did not spend much time pondering it. A few months later, when Joe was closer to three years of age, I realized Joe had a penchant for organization. Everything had a place, and everything needed to be in its place.

As with many (if not most) autistic children, Joe did not truly talk until he was three years old. For the most part, he lived in his own world. He occupied himself with objects around the house - his toys and other items that caught his eye. He seemed content, playing alone and not interacting with other children. To be honest, I was relieved when he was happy so I let him stay in his world. He would come to me at times to show me something such as a toy he had just noticed before retreating into his world.

Joe Being Joe

At about two years old, Joe taught himself to read using his alphabet blocks. Over time, I realized he loved to organize literally everything, which is an obsessive-compulsive behavior common to autistic toddlers, children, and adults, and I would sit on the floor next to him and organize. I would take his alphabet blocks and put them in order while saying each letter and the color of the letter. Soon he started to repeat the letter and color after me. He quickly learned the alphabet organization and would put the blocks in order himself. He really liked this activity and would get upset if his blocks were out of order. Everything in his room had a place and needed to stay in its place, and he would notice the smallest detail. When family and friends visited, inadvertently someone would move one of Joe's blocks. He would become extremely stressed and quickly put it where it belonged. After he fixed it, he was happy until the next time someone put something out of place. <u>This was a clue: repetitive activity encourages *serotonin* development and calms anxiety in autistic people.</u>

Exploring Outside the Home
Because I didn't drive at that time, I would take Joe for walks and bus rides. Joe would look around and spot a letter, identifying its name and color. He was so cute. He would beam. After Joe knew his letters and colors well, I began to say the word that he was looking at. Incredibly quickly, he began to recognize the words. He would point to them and say the word. He did not do this for the reward of my saying "good" or "great" because most of the time he did not seem to notice I was there or that anyone else was around. He was just engrossed in the letters he saw and the words he recognized. I was having a grand time with him. It was so interesting watching him evolve and learning new information. Learning letters and words seemed to click with Joe, and he quickly went from letters and colors to words and sentences. However, he still did not communicate well verbally. He repeated sentences that were in books without generating his own. Later, I learned that repeating not generating sentences is a useful method of diagnosing autistic children. Autistic children can repeat sentences and phrases called *echolalia* but seem to

have difficulty verbally generating thoughts.

Story Time

Joe loved story time. Every night, I would read a story to him. We needed to read the same book for weeks or months at a time. Interestingly, he was just as captivated by the words as the pictures. He memorized all his favorite books, especially the ones I read to him at bedtime. I realized this one night when he wanted to read a book that was upside down. Joe was able to read the story with precision. Many autistic children and adults have exceptional memories. Joe could remember everything anyone would say. He would repeat it word for word. That is not to say that he understood what was said and what he was repeating. After reading the same book for quite a while, Joe would notice a new book that I had laid out on a table and would want to read it. So then, we were able to read a new book and in time began to develop his personal library which he, of course, immediately began to organize. We had the most well-organized house in the neighborhood. His toys were in a particular order in his toy box. The blocks were in alphabetical order in the corner of his room. His books were neatly piled on his bed. Plastic colored balls and triangles were carefully placed on the windowsills. It was a mess to others but it was wonderfully organized to Joe. That was fine with me. I had previously tried to change things and realized that it was not worth the trouble. Joe would become too stressed when anything in the house was out of his designated place. No one understood Joe. I don't know that I understood him, either. I just took time to find out what worked and what didn't work with him. Honestly, that's really all I cared about. Joe loved to learn. He loved to organize his belongings. He was happy exploring, learning, and organizing. Why in the world would I want to change that? It is when I am remembering some of these experiences when Joe was a toddler that I wish I had a time machine so I could relive them.

The Autistic Difference: *Toddler*
• *Autonomy: "I'll Do It"---Erikson*

Motivating Movement
Some autistic toddlers may be content to sit idly locked in their own worlds. This behavior will inhibit learning and a positive progression through the life stages. The information a caregiver has gathered regarding the likes and dislikes and degree of sights and sounds that the infant can tolerate will be of essential value in the toddler stage. Using this information, the parents of autistic toddlers can set up environments to enhance their motivation to step out of their world and pay more attention to what is around them.

Set the Stage
Allowing the toddler to feed themselves, no matter how messy it can become, or allowing the toddler to bathe him/herself will help initiate the sense of autonomy. Some autistic toddlers will automatically begin to demand this autonomy, some will not. Encouraging autistic toddlers who are not motivated toward autonomy will help them to slowly begin to take steps to performing some daily activities for themselves.

Since developing autonomy is vital for future development, it is imperative for parents of autistic toddlers to motivate them to become as autonomous as possible. Autonomy itself relies on a toddler's developing trust in him/herself, whether they are autistic or not. As the infant develops trust in others for their care, the toddler must develop trust in his/her own abilities in this second stage.

Trust in Self

This personal trust comes from using one's body for exploring and experimenting. The toddler, especially the autistic toddler, must know what he/she is capable of accomplishing. Encouraging the autistic toddler to wash and brush teeth are important activities that allow a toddler to begin to know his/her own body and what it can do for him/her. Eating, washing, and brushing teeth develop muscle control that leads to the ability to further explore and experiment.

The Autistic Difference: _Toddler_
• *Obtain information through the senses, importance of movement, language development, fantasy, imagination*
• *Understand only one perspective of an item at a time---Piaget*

Redecorating the Home

This stage is the perfect time to begin "redecorating" the entire home of an autistic toddler with colorful, unbreakable objects that will motivate him or her to explore the environment and interact with those objects. Sometimes caregivers of autistic toddlers need to present these colorful objects to the toddler by actually putting the object in the toddler's hands.

Knowing the toddler's likes and dislikes will help parents to choose which colorful objects to place around the home. Getting to know what the autistic toddler can tolerate is one of the most important factors in helping an autistic toddler begin to explore his/her environment.

Self-Esteem, Self-Worth---Cooley

Toddlers, like infants, absorb the feelings of other especially feelings regarding themselves. Toddlers usually experience more people in their lives than infants bringing more feelings about them to be expressed. Toddlers not only absorb feeling from family members, immediate and extended, they now also absorb feelings of a wider variety of people such as day care employees. Awareness of how toddlers respond to each of these new people in their lives gives information as to how the toddler responds to the beliefs of the new entries into their lives.

Needs Based Motivation---Maslow

As toddlers venture out in exploration, safety becomes an increasing issue. The 2nd need in Maslow's hierarchy is safety as it is vital to ensure an environment that encourages exploration with is the hallmark of toddlerhood which lays the foundation for continued learning.

Abilities Based Motivation---Bandura

As toddlers explore, they discover what their bodies can and cannot do. A safe environment and a responsive caregiver enable a toddler to experiment with what they can't do to perfect their abilities. Ensuring a safe environment and encouragement for exploration ensures a growing sense of toddler ability.

CHAPTER 8

Joe's Adventures Begin

Preschool

High Hopes

The preschool stage held much promise for us. Joe and I had explored together, and he learned a lot about himself and his environment. He had learned to write his letters, colors, name, and address. He could identify many animals, the sounds they made and some of their behaviors. The next big adventure for him was preschool, and he began it with excitement in his soul. I shared in his excitement. Joe loved preschool but he marched to a different drummer, and his teacher did not appreciate Joe's unique drumbeat. Preschool shined a bright light on his differences, and provided a small taste of what was to come in primary and elementary school.

Insights on Preschool Age

Preschool includes the ages of 3-5 and is when children want to initiate activities on their own. They develop skills and language. Fantasy, imagination and understanding symbolism is usually prominent at this stage. Preschool is a time of significant change in a child's developmental growth, ideally for the better. This is the time when children step out into the world without parents in close proximity to protect them. In the previous stage, toddlers experiment and explore their environment. They develop ways to cope with their environment and become more confident in their ability to learn new tasks and capabilities. The toddler stage is a set up for the preschool stage in which children leave the protective comfort of their home and family and enter into a world filled with strangers, teachers, and other children.

Successful toddler experiences with exploring and learning are vital for a successful experience in preschool with strangers—not parents—in authority and with unfamiliar children rather than with family. In traditional preschool, children learn the important lesson of being somewhat on their own. Preschool children learn to obey rules and learn to share with other children.

Preschool and Autism

These preschool elements are difficult for autistic preschoolers. They don't engage in the same ways as non-autistic preschoolers. Because preschool children are starting out on their own, initiative is being developed. Children will begin to perform activities differently than they did at home simply because the environment is different, with different rules and expected behaviors. This is a natural and important lesson for children to learn. They are learning to adapt to new environments and new people with different personalities, temperaments, and expectations. This stage, however, can be a little difficult for our autistic children who tend to dislike change and unfamiliar environments. Difficult for most people, change is dramatically difficult for autistic children. Autistic children quite often perceive the world much differently than non-autistic children due to their intense focus on some objects or situations in the environment to the exclusion of other objects and situations. These circumstances are difficult for the autistic child and also for the teacher unfamiliar with the characteristics of autism.

Life with Joe: Achieving Initiative
I remember Joe's preschool experience with both laughter and horror. His very young and inexperienced but hopeful preschool teacher was perplexed by Joe. She viewed him as being completely incapable of being a functional part of a group because Joe had difficulty following directions and could not do activities in the same ways as the other preschoolers. Preschool was just a precursor of the problems ahead. If I could change one aspect and only one aspect of the education system, I would change the way teachers and other school personnel understand and treat special needs children. I dream that someday education professionals will see the beauty and intelligence of autistic and special needs children.

Through the eyes of autistic children, I have seen the world differently. Autistic children have helped me see the beauty in a piece of tree bark, for instance. They do not just see the bark. They see evidence of life. This might sound unimportant, but through them I have been given the opportunity to see the world from a different perspective, a perspective more open to possibilities. In not seeing these incredible qualities of autistic and special needs children, school professionals are missing a world of wonder and fascination. Teachers like Joe's preschool instructor deprive themselves and the children of infinite possibilities.

So Far So Good

Up to this point, Joe progressed in his development pretty well. He trusted me, he trusted himself, he explored easily, and he had learned to communicate verbally. He seemed happy... until he started preschool. I agreed with family and friends that he needed socialization and thought preschool would be a great venue for socialization. I may have been wrong about this one. Joe had a terrific time but his teacher didn't. Joe played class games, "Joe's way" which rarely followed the rules. He sang songs with his own words, not those taught by the teacher. That was fine with me. It was second nature to me by this time. I thought Joe was a brilliant and interesting kid. However, I soon realized I was one of the only ones, if not the only one, who thought so.

Inexperience and Misunderstanding

His teacher seemed to like young children. She liked to play games and sing songs with them. But I don't think she was ready for a preschooler like Joe. Once when I was observing the class, I had the opportunity to watch Joe in action. The class was playing Duck, Duck, Goose. Joe watched the children run around outside the circle of sitting children. He began to laugh, got up, and also ran around the circle of children, tapping each on the head. He paid no attention to the teacher who told him to sit and wait his turn. I picked him up and sat him back in the circle of children. That lasted about a minute. He again stood up and began to run around the circle laughing, having a grand time. No matter what I said to him nor what the teacher told him, he did his own thing. This upset the teacher terribly. She tried so hard to get me to take him out of her class. Unfortunately, this was basically the only source of socialization for Joe. I was not going to do as she requested. There were no other young children in our immediate neighborhood with whom he could play. And, very important to me, he smiled when he went to preschool.

A Turning Point

At preschool graduation the teacher had the children sing, "Rubber Duckie." They prepared and practiced a little dance routine to go along with the song. Each had their own little, yellow rubber duckie. They looked so cute up on the stage singing and dancing. Joe was adorable. He was beaming, smiling from ear to ear. There was only one problem. Joe was doing his own Rubber Duckie song and his own dance routine. I was pleased he was somewhat paying attention to the music and the other children around him. The teacher came up to me at the end of the graduation ceremony and said that Joe ruined the performance and the entire graduation ceremony. She did not want him in her class ever again. I was truly heartbroken since I had such high hopes. I took the blame for his behavior upon myself. I didn't know why Joe behaved the way he did. All I knew was that I couldn't seem to change him. We never returned to the preschool. We did our own thing. Although it was a bit isolating, I was beginning to march to my own drumbeat, too. Joe was four years old. Was there no one tolerant of the behavior of a young child who stood out from the crowd? I would no longer be silent. I would advocate for Joe. Things were changing inside of me. Not huge changes yet but changes, nevertheless. For the most part, Joe was a quiet child. He did not have tantrums nor did he exhibit aggressive behavior. He never instigated problems with others. He was content to do his own thing. He was somewhat oblivious of the world around him and so created his own world. I was beginning to think that this was a good thing for him. He just made the best of life. I thought Joe was normal and everyone else just didn't understand. I'm not sure what that says about me but that was the way things were. Joe was Joe. Why didn't he sleep? Why didn't he talk? Why didn't he play in the same way as the other children? On and on it went, and it only got worse as Joe progressed through school.

The Autistic Difference: Preschool
• *Initiative: starting projects---Erikson*

Preschool or Not
Attending traditional preschool helps develop a child's social skills. Parents of autistic preschoolers must take into consideration the level of interaction and also their children's developmental capabilities. For the autistic child, the preschool experience can help or hinder future school-based experiences.

Socialization
Fortunately, preschool is not the only socialization activity that might be available. If the autistic preschooler is adept at interacting with others, especially children of their own age, then a traditional preschool might be a productive experience. If, however, the autistic preschooler is not comfortable engaging with others, then different activities should be considered. There are physical education classes geared toward preschoolers, including autistic preschoolers, where the focus is on the activity itself as opposed to interaction with others—for example, a Mommy and Me class or swim lessons.

In these places, interaction skills are being developed because the autistic preschooler is required to pay attention to the instructor and accomplish a deed.

The main goal of this stage of development is becoming comfortable with others besides parents, caregivers, and extended family. This is preparation for the elementary school experience. The most important goal of this stage is allowing children the freedom to initiate activities, to choose and become involved in activities. The preschool environment gives the child the necessary adjustment time to consider skills and engage in activities that help in mastering those skills.

Some preschools will have very structured activities. This is not necessarily a bad thing for the autistic preschooler, but be sure to allow the preschooler time at home to experience the freedom to initiate activities they desire to do. Ideally, parents, caregivers, and extended family engage in these activities with the preschooler when invited to do so.

The Autistic Difference: Toddler
* *Language development, fantasy, imagination, understand only one perspective of an item at a time*
* *Need hands-on activities to learn, classifying, trial-and-error problem-solving---Piaget*

I Don't See That
At this stage, a child, autistic or not, can only conceptualize **one** aspect of an item or situation at a time. This the normal way of understanding the world from the point of view of a preschooler. But this understanding of objects and items in the environment still can cause confusion for preschoolers, especially autistic preschoolers, who commonly have difficulty with language development.

Learning Style

Everyone has a preferred way of learning or taking in information. Because autistic preschoolers have difficulty communicating, it is more helpful to try explanations in various forms—visually, verbally, or physically with acting them out. In this way, parents and teachers can help autistic preschoolers to better understand objects and concepts in their environment. With time and practice, the preschooler will eventually begin to understand more than one aspect of an item at a time.

Sharing?

Another area of concern for preschoolers is the concept of sharing. Sharing is a difficult concept for children at this age, and it's not an inherent skill. It must be taught with patience and tolerance. According to Piaget, preschoolers at this stage believe everyone thinks the same way they do (e.g., If I want something, then everyone wants me to have it.) This preschool thought process does not align with the concept of sharing. Because the autistic child has difficulty with verbal communication, the concept of sharing may be more effectively explained by using facial expressions, drawings, and dolls.

Empathy!

Too many people, professionals included, mistakenly believe that autistic children and adults do not feel empathy. They do. They just have more difficulty expressing emotions and empathy. It is never too early to begin teaching preschoolers to be aware of feelings. It takes some effort on the part of parents and teachers to couple verbal explanations of feelings with facial expressions and ask them to explain their own feelings. The end result, however, is a more compassionate and empathetic child, which is worth the effort.

Self-Esteem and Self-Worth---Cooley
If children are not doing well in preschool, a parent-teacher meeting can be helpful, especially if both parties truly listen to and respect each other's specialized information and knowledge.

Needs Based Motivation---Maslow
Autistic preschoolers often are resistant to change. They may want to stay in the familiar rather than charge into the unknown. A sense of safety and belonging assists in motivating autistic preschoolers in making the changes they need to make.

Abilities Based Motivation---Bandura
Encourage children to try out new ways of doing familiar activities. In this way, children discover new abilities within themselves and develop new skills to use in school.

Know the types of activities that motivate your students to continue learning. This knowledge of their likes and dislikes, interests and abilities will help in all stages of development.

CHAPTER 9

Joe Knows Stranger Danger

Primary School

Some Answers

Joe was six years old and in primary school when his pediatrician diagnosed him with autism. We finally learned the reason behind Joe's different behavior. Still, a true understanding of Joe's autism eluded teachers and other school staff since most people, teachers, and other professionals alike knew little to nothing about it. At this point, I did not know if the diagnosis was helpful or hurtful to our situation. I realized the danger of a society that does not understand differences in children. There was no real help. We had a diagnosis but I was still alone in trying to assist my son to function in society.

Insights on Primary School Age

Primary school includes the ages of 4-6 and is again focused on skill and language development, and has the child wanting to initiate activities on their own. Just as toddlerhood prepares the child for preschool, preschool prepares the child for kindergarten, which, in turn, prepares the child for elementary school. It is truly a developmental step-by-step process toward adulthood. Primary school readies young children for the more academic aspect of school life. Primary school children are required to spend more time in quiet activities, such as reading and writing. However, primary school still includes physical activities such as games, drawing, and coloring that are not a daily part of third, fourth, and fifth grade. Children are being carefully weaned in primary school from an active environment to a more quiet, passive academic school environment.

This is difficult enough for any young child. However, it is extremely difficult for the autistic primary school child who abhors change and tends to repeat activities long after an activity warrants. The difference between the preschool and primary school environments is immense for the autistic young child, who knows school as a place for learning and play. While this may seem like a miniscule change to parents and teachers, it is overwhelming to the autistic primary school child because perseveration makes him/her unable to change behavior patterns easily. Parents need to prepare their autistic young children for this change.

Life with Joe: Achieving Initiative

The summer before Joe started kindergarten, I encouraged him to practice writing his name and address. The hours of practice would not have been necessary but for a bout with encephalitis several months earlier, which he contracted on a family picnic. It was the year in which mosquitos had created an epidemic and Joe was one of their victims.

Making Matters Worse
Joe was terribly ill with a high fever of 106 degrees. When the fever subsided, Joe was dazed for days losing much of his coordination. He had trouble eating, drinking, dressing, and writing and was left with an awkward gait. It was probably not the ideal time to begin kindergarten.

Before the encephalitis, Joe had been able to write his name, address, letters, numbers, and colors. After the illness, it was almost impossible for him. I drilled him on the skills but looking back, this was probably not a good idea. I should have waited for his body's coordination to return. I just did not know if it would return so I had him practice over and over. I should have just let him play. That may have helped him heal faster and more completely. It took a few years for Joe's coordination to be fully restored but some aspects, such as his walking gait, took many more years to return to more normal functioning.

Starting Kindergarten
Joe's first day of kindergarten dawned with promise. He was looking forward to it. Joe loved to read, and I told him every day that he would read in school. That first day, we walked to school, looking forward to the new adventure of reading and learning. Things couldn't be any better. Joe got in line with the other children and smiled as he walked into the school building with the kindergarten teacher and the other students. I started to cry. I would miss the days we had together playing, reading, and

walking. He was growing up, and I felt the loss. I remember thinking the teacher was a professional and educated in ways of working with young children. I was confident that she would know how to help Joe when he was in need. The first day of kindergarten might have been Joe's last happy kindergarten day.

Sounds Familiar
His teacher was much like his preschool teacher. The children needed to sit at their desks doing exactly what the teacher wanted them to do. It wasn't that Joe refused to follow directions. He just wasn't paying attention to the teacher while she was giving the directions. He was absorbed in his own world - visually exploring the new environment, getting up from his desk at will to touch items on shelves - basically, he was being Joe. Of course, this did not go over well with his teacher.

Almost immediately, the teacher contacted me to say Joe was not ready for school. She thought that he had some kind of problem. I mentioned he had had encephalitis and had lost his coordination recently. I said he was getting better, would eventually fit in. I guess I was dreaming. School life did not get better.

The kindergarten teacher was frustrated and was beginning to show anger toward me. She called me often. One day while at school, Joe tried to pick up a pencil he dropped on the floor. Due to his lack of coordination, he fell. The children laughed at Joe and teased him. The teacher allowed them to tease Joe so often that Joe spent much of his time hiding under his desk. The teacher believed Joe's hiding under his desk was a problem. I agreed with her. However, my solution to the problem of Joe's hiding under his desk was to stop the other children from teasing him. That attitude did not go over well.

Field Trips

Joe was not allowed to go on the first kindergarten field trip. The teacher cited safety problems with Joe since he did not pay attention to her. For subsequent field trips, the teacher said she would assign a parent to be with him for the trip. I was a little uncomfortable with the idea of the teacher discussing Joe and his behavior with other parents so I didn't allow him to go. One evening, the teacher called and asked if I would accompany Joe on the field trip. I did. I went on two trips with the class. Joe was fine. He held my hand when appropriate and did not cause problems for the group. When adults paid attention to Joe's needs, he was fine.

A Problem?

Because Joe spent so much time under his desk, the teacher asked to have Joe tested by the school psychologist. I agreed. I knew Joe was different, just didn't know why. Testing might clear up the mystery. I actually was looking forward to the results.
The school psychologist planned to take Joe out of class one day and conduct the testing. I thought this would be fine. Well, it would have been if we had prepared Joe properly. It was as much my fault as it was the fault of the teacher and the psychologist. I assumed they knew what they were doing so I did not question the process. I could not have been more wrong. The week before the testing, a police officer came into the kindergarten class and spoke to the children about "stranger danger." It must have been the rhyming words that caught Joe's attention. He listened to the officer. He paid attention and learned that he was not

supposed to go anywhere with strangers.

Whose Problem?

Well, the very next week, the psychologist came into the classroom and approached Joe. He was a stranger, and Joe remembered the warning. The psychologist wanted to take Joe away - out of class. Joe was terrified and screamed and cried. He refused to go out of the classroom with the psychologist, even when the teacher encouraged him to do so. He was frightened and spent the rest of the day sitting quietly under his desk. Needless to say, there was no testing that day.

The teacher and psychologist contacted me to make sure I understood this behavior was unacceptable and proved Joe had severe problems. That did not sit well with me. I wanted to know why Joe screamed and cried. It was so unlike Joe. He was usually friendly to people. I wasn't sure if I had ever heard Joe scream. I had many questions for both the teacher and the psychologist.

Oh, That's the Problem

I discovered that the police officer had been in Joe's class a week before the appointment with the psychologist. I also found out that the psychologist never observed Joe in the classroom and never showed Joe that he knew the teacher. The bottom line is that no one made the testing process a safe event for Joe. He was frightened. A non-autistic five-year-old probably would have obeyed and gone with the stranger given the teacher's direction. However, Joe was autistic. He protested being taken away by a stranger and away from his safe environment. I didn't understand why the teacher and school psychologist couldn't comprehend this. Joe's behavior made sense to me. It did not sit well with the teacher and the psychologist. They kept saying that I was in denial. DENIAL?! Denial of what?!? They frightened him. What was he supposed to do? Just meekly go away with a stranger? Actually, I was proud of him for doing what he did.

Fixing the Problem

I mentioned this incident to the principal. The next school year, the kindergarten teacher was no longer at the school. The principal, through discussions with other parents and teachers, had become aware of a few of her missteps and she was asked to leave. That was when I first realized the untapped power parents hold as advocates for their children.

The kindergarten experience with the school psychologist was traumatic for Joe. He was frightened. Joe knew only that the school psychologist was a stranger and it frightened him. Joe did exactly what he should have done. The fact that the professionals did not understand is fairly unforgivable to me. They should have known better and prepared Joe for the experience.

Continue Fixing

A couple of years later, while I was employed in the school's learning center, I worked with a fifth-grade girl. She came to me one morning and said she was afraid. I sat with her and asked her to tell me what she feared. After much urging, she told me that her teenage male babysitter, "went to the bathroom inside of her." She was afraid she would get sick. My first thought was sex abuse. The school psychologist (yes, the same one) refused to work with the girl for counseling. He said her mother was a "whore" and the girl would grow up to be a "whore," so she needed to just get used to it. This caused just about everyone in the school to cringe in horror. The school psychologist was fired. I felt good about that. He, along with the kindergarten teacher, proved to be incompetent in their positions. Joe and I, without fully realizing it, were beginning to make our impact on the future of education for special needs children.

The Autistic Difference*: Primary School*
- *Industry: Completing Projects Successfully---Erikson*

Communication
Autistic primary school children may spend much of the class time in their own world. They also may have difficulty in communicating their needs and in heeding directions depending on where they are on the autism spectrum. It is not that they cannot learn these tasks, it just may be more difficult due to their sensitivity to excessive visual and auditory stimuli. It is imperative that kindergarten teachers are aware of the communication level of their autistic students. Th is responsibility falls on the parents. Th ere is no one better than parents to accurately inform the teacher about an autistic child's level of communication skills and ability to interact with others and for how long.

Parents/Caregivers
At every stage of their child's life, parents can create activities to help their autistic child better assimilate. Th is stage is no different. Caregivers can create games that reflect the kindergarten classroom. Parents also can play games like Simon Says so the autistic child learns to pay attention, listen to instructions, and follow those instructions.

Goal
The goal of this stage is initiating activities. Primary school children love to start projects. They do not always need to think of them on their own. The projects and activities that parents and teachers initiate can work well. Parents of autistic primary school children can do a lot to help their children be comfortable in the kindergarten environment. Consistent contact with teachers and school personnel is important to assure that their autistic children are not only feeling comfortable in primary school but also are able to reach their potential.

The Autistic Difference: Primary School
• Language development, fantasy, imagination, understand only one perspective of an item at a time
• Need hands-on activities to learn, trial-and-error problem solving---Piaget

Preparing
Preparing the autistic child for this change in structure is highly recommended. Setting up a classroom-like experience for the child at home is a way for the child to become familiar with the new required behavior. It will allow the child to have the physical and emotional energy to focus on academics.

Activities that Help
It's important to remember that autistic children have as many, if not more, levels of academic potential as non-autistic children. Since one of the main areas of a child's focus at this stage is fantasy and imagination, these can be used to an advantage to assist an autistic child in learning the requirements of new classroom behaviors and learning experiences. Reading stories about children at school may be helpful. Drawing him/herself in

a desk, in the classroom and hanging it on a wall can be a reminder of the new behavior.

The most important factor is knowing your child and his/her levels of communication and interaction and conveying this information to teachers and other school authorities.

Self-Esteem, Self-Worth---Cooley

Many autistic children have a higher level of anxiety than other children. Some situations and activities that may seem harmless and fun can be seen as dangerous and frightening to an autistic child. The autistic child may take more time just surveying the situation to determine the danger level. Understanding and encouragement are needed.

Needs Based Motivation---Maslow

Patience with children who are processing information more slowly than others; helps them build self-confidence.

Modeling patience t autistic children helps them to be motivated to continue difficult tasks they need to learn.

Abilities Based Motivation---Bandura

An environment rich with color, books, and writing and drawing materials entices a child to explore and engage in that environment, which is important for the learning process.

CHAPTER 10

Joe Becomes a Teacher

Elementary School

Challenges and Opportunities

Elementary school had its ups and downs for Joe. One of the ups was his friendship with a boy his age who lived down the block from us. Joe and his friend were together on the weekends during the school year and every day in the summers. Joe's friend could ride a bike so he wanted to learn to ride a bike. He learned despite his somewhat awkward coordination, a leftover from his bout with encephalitis. Both boys were quiet, gentle souls who seemed to understand each other's feelings. Joe's friend was one of the truly wonderful experiences of elementary school. Even though they no longer are in touch, Joe has never forgotten him.

Insights on Elementary School Age

This stage includes ages 5 - 12 with a focus on action, and competence; learning through action, and solving problems through trial and error. Children also learn *seriation*, enjoying classification through collecting items such as comic books and model cars.

Elementary school is not only about academic education, reading, writing, and arithmetic. In this stage children begin to use information in new and different ways. Not only do children learn to read and write, they first _learn to read_, then they _read to learn_. In other words, the emphasis is no longer on just learning to read, the emphasis is now on comprehension.

This is a stage where the children are learning to investigate, research, and use information to develop a project. In California, for example, fourth grade students learn about California geographic regions and missions. They not only read and research information about the state and go on field trips, they also are required to develop a project using the assembled information. In today's world, this project can involve many facets, including technology.

More Than Academics

The absorption of knowledge is not the only aspect of education. The other aspect is on the skills children develop to use this knowledge and communicate it to others. However, elementary school is more than the learning of subject matter, using this information in creative ways and communicating this information to others. It also must focus on the development of self-confidence and self-esteem. The child in this stage needs to feel capable of learning new skills and presenting these abilities to others. He/she also needs to feel self-respect and attain the respect of others. This is the cognitive stage that allows children to begin to perceive the world as adults do. This is the stage in which children begin to reason, rationalize situations and events, and see the world as their parents and teachers see the world.

All of this takes time. It takes the time and energy of parents and teachers to set up the children's environment and experiences within that setting to assist children in learning new skills and using information creatively. This also develops self-esteem and self-confidence, attaining respect, and beginning to feel where their place in the world might be.

This stage goes beyond just thinking they want to be a fire fighter, astronaut, or teacher. Now, they are beginning to evaluate their skills and their ability to develop skills. They are better able to realistically perceive the evaluations of others regarding their abilities. They are steering away from fantasy desires toward more realistic expectations for what they will actually eventually do in society. They are going from the fantasy, imaginative, symbolic world of *preoperational* thought to a more realistic, rational evaluation of themselves.

The Adult's Role

The adults in their environment are needed to set up experiences in which the children not only learn about their developing skills but also learn to succeed. Feeling success is important in developing the motivation to continue the learning process. This includes experiences in which children may fail but also learn why they failed and how to change failure into success. This is a lesson that is ultimately most important. Its foundation is in the fact that the children feel confident enough in themselves to keep trying and to be motivated to keep trying. It is an important lesson at this age and throughout adulthood. Because autistic and other special needs children experience many difficulties in school, it is imperative that all that is necessary be done to keep their motivation for accomplishing activities as high as possible.

Their success in life depends on it.

Life with Joe: Achieving Industry

When Joe was seven years old, I was told by his neurologist that he would not be able to complete elementary and middle school. Instead, he would obtain a certificate of attendance because he was incapable of understanding and completing the schoolwork required to receive a diploma. Yes, school was difficult for him, but I truly believed that Joe was intelligent enough to complete the academic requirements of elementary and middle school.

My Remedy

When doing schoolwork at home with him, I would discuss the concepts presented in class. Joe always understood the concepts well once I related them to his interests.

In class, he was absorbing the information and could explain the concepts easily to me at home. It helped that we were discussing the concepts one-on-one with no interfering stimuli in the room. Joe could readily absorb information but had difficulty communicating that information, especially in a noisy classroom. If I knew then what I know now, I might have homeschooled Joe. The major problems that Joe and I experienced were all related to school. Joe's problems began in primary school-kindergarten, first and second grades. Joe did not fit in. He was a "square peg" of a child in a "round hole" of a school.

Teacher's Role

The good news is that in primary school, the teachers were more tolerant of student differences. In first grade, Joe attended a developmental class. It was for children with special needs. The teacher would contact me often, but there was little to no frustration in her voice when she spoke of Joe's behavior. She was grateful that Joe was quiet and read most of the time. He did not cause disruptions in class and did not quarrel with the other students. He paid attention to her at times but still did not complete assignments. He began worksheet assignments but rarely completed them. He seemed to lose interest in them after filling in a few items. I believe he was bored with the worksheets. He knew the information and did not understand why he needed to communicate this through them.

In second grade, Joe was returned to a traditional classroom environment because the school did not have a developmental second grade. This teacher also was patient and tolerant of Joe's differences and said that Joe caused no problems in the class. He just did not join in classroom activities and did little of the assignments except for those that were not worksheets. He completed or almost completed assignments that required drawings and storytelling. That was a big improvement over the previous year.

The Beginning of Knowing

This teacher wanted Joe's father and I to visit a family therapist. She thought that something in the family dynamics was affecting Joe's behavior. Joe's father and I went to the appointment. The therapist told us our marriage problems were the core issue with Joe's behavior. Well, he was right about the problems blooming in our marriage, but I believe he didn't consider the fact that Joe's autism could possibly be an important reason why our marriage had problems.

One positive event resulted from this meeting: I discussed this issue with Joe's pediatrician who, after examining Joe, said for the first time that he believed Joe was autistic. I had never heard of the disorder and had difficulty researching it. I discovered a nearby university hospital, Loyola University Medical Center, that was beginning to do research on autism and made an appointment to see the neurologist in charge of the research.

Dr. H. and Caffeine

Dr. H. was a child psychologist from France who also believed Joe was autistic. However, at this stage of her research, she had no significant treatment to offer. We continued to see Dr. H. for another year. Before we stopped seeing her, she said the only thing she could advise was to have Joe drink coffee with cocoa every morning. Coffee especially with cocoa contains caffeine. Joe refused to drink it at first and did not start drinking it until middle school, when it worked wonders.

We all know the energy charge we get from caffeine. However, caffeine works in the opposite way when given to hyperactive children or children who have difficulty focusing. Caffeine seems to help autistic children be calmer, more focused. Who knew a cup of coffee was a miracle drug for children who need help to focus?

Dr. Z, Another Ally

Dr. Z., an educational psychologist recommended by Dr. H., realized there were serious problems in my marriage without me saying a word. She understood I was on my own working with Joe to resolve these issues. Joe's father did not come to our parent meetings with Dr. Z., so sometimes she would stop by our home. Even then, Joe's father wouldn't speak with her about Joe. I remember sitting on the stairs in our home talking with her while he stayed in the basement. She spoke of professional techniques to help Joe and told me she believed that Joe's father might never be ready or capable of becoming a true partner in terms of helping Joe. It was a special moment between us. She cared so much for Joe and me. We worked together until Joe graduated from middle school. She was our advocate. She was the first person I would call when I needed advice or help with Joe in school. She was always there for us. As elementary school progressed, the teachers seemed much less tolerant in working with student differences and special needs.

Teacher's Insight

Fortunately, the exception was Joe's third grade teacher. Joe's third grade teacher noticed his immense knowledge of geography and his ability to focus on maps in a way he could not focus on other subjects. She came up with an innovative solution and asked me if Joe would like to teach geography to the class. I thought it was a great idea. Since Joe did not fit in, I thought that his teacher was right to show the other students that Joe had value. Joe's teaching career began at eight years old. His teacher would give him a country to talk about and Joe would take it from there. Joe's knowledge earned him the respect of the other students. They stopped teasing him. From third grade all the way through eighth grade, no one bullied Joe. Joe's problems stopped coming from the other students; instead, his problems came from some of the teachers.

Teachers' Intolerance

Joe's third grade teacher was very tolerant. That was not the case with his fourth and fifth grade teachers. For example, Joe could not write cursive. He printed his letters and words in the same way as he saw them on paper and in books. No matter how we tried, Joe could not write in cursive. Interestingly, many other autistic children cannot write in cursive; there seems to be a motor control issue with their ability to move their hands in a flowing manner. For these children, computers, tablets, and other electronic devices are a godsend. Unfortunately, computers and tablets did not exist in schools at the time Joe was in elementary school. Joe's fourth grade teacher would not accept any of his work if it was not in cursive so Joe received no grades for doing the assignments that he completed. I contacted Joe's educational psychologist, Dr. Z., and asked her to write a letter to the teacher and to the principal explaining that Joe was not capable of writing in cursive. The teacher would not accept the information in the letter. Dr. Z. then contacted Joe's pediatrician and asked him to write a letter to the teacher and principal regarding Joe's inability to write in cursive.

Yet Another Ally

I was surprised when the pediatrician also met in person with the principal on Joe's behalf. Well, that worked. The teachers and principal finally accepted the fact that Joe was not capable of writing in cursive. I found out months later that the pediatrician had a child with learning disabilities and all of his five children attended the same school as Joe. Lucky for us, the pediatrician was also a friend of Dr. Z. He ended the war of cursive writing. Joe printed his assignments, and his teachers said nothing more about it. The experience Joe had in third grade helped him feel confidence in himself. It took one teacher with insight and tolerance to set up an experience for Joe that provided him with a sense of self-confidence and self-respect and earned the respect of others. One teacher. Yes, the fourth and fifth grade experiences were difficult but they seemed easier for Joe to bear after the previous year. He knew he could teach and so did the other students.

The Autistic Difference: Elementary School
• *Physical activities for learning---Erikson*

<u>Interest Area</u>
Like all children, autistic children are very motivated to learn and capable of learning. If we carefully observe an autistic child, we will notice the intense focus they have when involved with objects or events in their interest areas.

The first and foremost requirement for parents and teachers of autistic elementary school children is to be aware of the child's interests. It is through their interests that parents and teachers not only can enter the world of the autistic child but also help the child focus on the task at hand.

The objective at this stage is to assist the autistic child in focusing on the project and completing it successfully. This can be difficult for a child who is easily distracted, but we know that an autistic child can spend hours on projects that interest them. The goal for parents and teachers is to transfer the intense focus from the activities that most interest the child to activities in school.

As autistic children become more involved in classroom activities and complete them successfully, they will become motivated to initiate and complete the next project or goal. This process is vital for future learning and achievement.

The Autistic Difference: Elementary School
• *Physical activities, need hands-on activities to learn, classifying, trial-and-error problem-solving---Piaget*

<u>Importance of the Physical</u>
The need for physical activities to learn, classify, and notice subtle details of objects is similar for autistic elementary school-age children. Due to their inability to remain engaged with their environment, autistic children may experience problems in sequencing and classification. Once they can focus on a cartoon strip, for example, they will be able to conceptualize the story and then be able to put the cartoon sections in order.

Assisting autistic children in accomplishing the tasks of this stage means helping them focus on the task at hand. In some situations, this is easier said than done. However, it is vital not only for their future learning but also for motivating them to learn.

Self-Esteem, Self-Worth---Cooley
Parent/teacher meetings are crucial for to acquire personal information from parents about what children do at home.

The same is true of parents, who need to obtain information about what their children are doing in school and the attitude of teachers toward the autistic child.

Needs Based Motivation---Maslow

Elementary school sparks an interest in social activities such as clubs and sports which entails a sense of belonging. Be aware of activities that will interest the autistic student while ensuring a sense of safety.

Abilities Based Motivation---Bandura

Involve elementary-aged children in activities that are age and skill appropriate.

Knowing a child's interests and skill levels helps develop appropriate activities children can complete successfully and be motivated to initiate another project or learning experience is vital in establishing a lifelong motivation to accomplish goals.

CHAPTER 11

Joe Says, "Coffee with Cocoa, Please"

Middle School

Change is Good

Middle school dawned with bright expectations. Joe left the known, routine elementary school environment of one teacher in one classroom, for the different and possibly unsettling middle school environment of multiple teachers in multiple classrooms. I feared this situation would be problematic for Joe. However, the change from elementary school to middle school was good for him. The majority of his teachers were younger men and seemed to take his different behavior in stride. They rarely called regarding Joe's not paying attention in class. Parent/teacher conferences were more pleasurable than disturbing. Joe actually did some of his assignments without much struggling. I wondered about the difference. Could it possibly have anything to do with the daily cup of coffee?

Insights on Middle School Age

Middle school includes ages 10 - 12 and focuses learning through action. Middle school is the threshold between childhood and adolescence. Middle schoolers are still children but look forward to being teenagers and engaging in social experimentation. Friends begin to replace family in importance. However, middle school children still need the involvement of parents and are just beginning to test the boundaries of what parents will allow. Middle school and preadolescence are the times in children's lives when they begin to waiver from the belief systems of their parents. This comes into full bloom in adolescence, the next stage of development. Preadolescence is the launching pad of the experimentation stage of adolescence, giving parents a glimmer of the adults, their children might become. The clues are endless, which makes this a busy and exciting time.

Life with Joe: Achieving Industry

Joe seemed to do better in grades six to eight. He was basically the same but his teachers were different. They worked with Joe, and it was a period of relative calm. Joe seemed more engaged in the school learning process. He began to pay a little more attention in classes and was able to do more homework. At the beginning of middle school, Joe's doctor again suggested giving him coffee with cocoa in the mornings to help him focus. The first time Joe tried it, he didn't like it. This time, however, I mixed the coffee with a premade cocoa mixture. Joe drank it and actually liked it. The caffeine seemed to help Joe pay attention in class a little more, and I didn't get as many complaints from teachers.

During Joe's middle school years, we still had parent conferences in which the teachers talked of Joe's struggles with paying attention in class and completing schoolwork. However, these meetings were more pleasant. His teachers seemed to have a sense of humor about his class behavior. They seemed genuinely pleased with Joe's progress.

Most teacher complaints had to do with the fact that Joe would occasionally put his head down on his desk and take a nap. Joe still did not fall asleep until about 2 a.m. He would be in bed at 9 p.m. but would read his beloved books and study his beloved maps. He was resting but not sleeping. This was a compromise that kept everyone sane.

The only time Joe's middle school teachers were upset by his naps was when he took naps during state testing. One evening, Joe's teacher called to tell me that Joe had taken a nap during his state math test. He said the nap would really impact Joe's score on the test. He also said that he'd, "like to wring Joe's neck." I didn't take offense. I knew the feeling. A few weeks later, the teacher again called with the results of the state math test. Joe had done very well, despite his nap! This situation was a learning experience for Joe's teachers, who realized that Joe was actually learning the information presented to him. The fact that he did little of his homework or classwork did not stop Joe from learning. The problem was Joe's inability to communicate that information to others. This behavior is not only common to autistic children, it is also common to other types of special needs children, especially those with auditory or verbal processing problems. Since Joe's teachers were beginning to understand he retained information, they had fewer negative reports about Joe's behavior.

Progress, but Joe is Still Joe

Sometimes, Joe would please his teachers by actually doing some classwork. For the most part, though, he was still in his own world. It was a world filled with maps - maps of the world and maps of the stars. His world consisted of atlases, books on countries, and books on the planets and the stars. He was content in his world, and his ability to focus on his maps and books was astonishing. *Extreme focus on an interest area is common for autistic children and adults alike.*

During a college course presentation, I explained this phenomenon to the professor and fellow students and showed pictures of Joe with his drawings of maps. I explained Joe had difficulty tying his shoes but could draw a map of a continent on a small, one-inch square slide. The students were fascinated. The professor mentioned that he had heard of this phenomenon, and I was intrigued. This meant that there were others like Joe out there. Someday, I hoped that I would meet them.

A Tiny Step Forward

I continued to use his maps and reference books to help him with his homework. I would relate his math problems to countries and continents and relate science to the natural resources of his beloved countries. That was the best, if not only way to get him to do his homework. I had to be creative about how to enter his world and coax him to do the necessary activities in our world. The most remarkable aspect about all of this was not only the level of focus Joe displayed with his interests but the level of contentment and satisfaction that showed on his face. Joe began to share some of his information with me while in elementary school and this continued in middle school. This was a new behavior for Joe.

Something had changed. It was not only my entering his world to get his attention, now he was drawing me into his world by leading me into his room and showing me his maps, books, and other information. He would glow when I commented on them. He especially was pleased when I asked questions and gave him the opportunity to tell me what he had learned. These were very special moments alone with my son. It would be years before he let anyone else into his world. I cherished those moments. And I learned a lot. I realized Joe had a *didactic* or photographic memory for everything he read and heard. He could recite word for word everything he had read, whether it was a page, a chapter, or an entire book. He could not tie his shoes, but he could draw maps exactly as they were presented in the atlas. He did not remember if he was hungry or not, but he could recite an entire book from memory. Joe was a lot of fun to have as a child.

The Marriage

As the problems with Joe seemed to lessen at school, the problems in my marriage continued to grow. Joe's father rarely came to teacher meetings. He rarely came home for dinner. He rarely interacted with Joe. Joe really did not know his father and, perhaps just as important, his father did not know Joe. They both missed out on a lot of wonderful experiences. In graduate school, I did research on the effects of children with invisible disabilities on family dynamics. Invisible disabilities are those disabilities such as autism that are not immediately apparent. What I discovered was astonishing. Statistics showed that more than 90% of families with children with invisible disabilities such as autism end in divorce. Our family eventually became one of those statistics. The divorce happened in 1980 when Joe was 14 years old. Now that there is a better understanding of differences and disabilities, and more assistance available, the statistics reflect some improvement.

Unfortunately, Joe's father passed away never knowing how special and truly wonderful his son is. Most of our family members still don't understand what Joe goes through on a daily basis. For some, the information is too overwhelming and uncomfortable. For others, ignorance is bliss. I'm not saying they don't love Joe. They just don't know him. I believe Joe would like family members to reach out to him, to enter his world. They would see Joe as he really is, a fascinating person.

The Autistic Difference: Middle School

• *Industry, ego identity, who am I?---Erikson*

Anxiety

Autistic middle schoolers also need to make realistic evaluations of their skills and abilities. However, parents, teachers, and coaches must take into account their children's level of anxiety. A great number of autistic children have high anxiety levels that hamper their ability to evaluate themselves without becoming upset and angry.

Extra Time

When beginning to learn a skill, an autistic child may need extra time since their anxiety can use up energy. They may need to repeat activities more often than other children in order to feel comfortable that the skill has been achieved. It depends on the level of focus the autistic child has for a particular activity.

Interests Again

Knowing the child's interests and past accomplishments helps parents and teachers successfully guide the autistic child in a more personal manner that accommodates their anxiety and inability to focus. Parents and teachers of autistic children should aim to know the child's level of achievement and understand their potential for anxiety and which types of activities cause them to feel overwhelmed. In this way, autistic children will be able to accomplish tasks successfully and feel the pleasure of success experienced by others.

The successful completion of tasks will motivate the autistic child as it does with the non-autistic child. This is significant since autistic children often do not experience success due to a lack of interaction with others in their environment.

The Autistic Difference: *Middle School*

• Physical Activities, Need hands-on activities to learn, trial-and-error problem-solving

• Abstract thinking, consequences of decisions into future, drop back to concrete thinking when stressed, anxious or ill---Piaget

Active Learning

For the autistic child, active, concrete learning is just as valuable as it is to a non-autistic child, maybe even more so. Considerations, of course, would include interest areas, anxiety levels, and the ability to focus in an active environment. Joining clubs that focus on the autistic child's interest area is a way to help develop socialization and practice learned skills.

Involvement

Some autistic children at this age are interested in sports. They may want to play the sport or be a member of the team in another capacity such as keeping score or handling statistics.

There also are online clubs that they can join. However, it is extremely important that parents monitor these types of activities as autistic children at this age can be vulnerable to predators of all sorts.

The most important aspect here is that the autistic child has ways to actively learn through specifically focused projects and field trips within and without school parameters. Parents/teachers can develop field experiences for their autistic child and others in the neighborhood. There are endless online virtual tours and academic experiences in which to take part. Educational and academic programs on the internet, when used wisely, can provide a wealth of opportunities for middle school autistic children.

Self-Esteem, Self-Worth---Cooley
Children at this age are transitioning from childhood to adolescence. They want to grow up but truly are still children. Their desire to grow up often sets them up for problems far beyond their years. Being involved in school activities, and knowing their friends helps when a problem arises before it seriously impacts the child's life.

Needs Based Motivation---Maslow
Socialization begins to become increasingly important for children at this stage. Even though they might ask parents and teachers to stay out of certain situations, they secretly do want and need input.

Abilities Based Motivation---Bandura
At this stage students are transitioning from concrete thinking to abstract thinking---beginning to cross the threshold into being

able to realistically understand future consequences of behavior.

Presenting information in several ways is important as is relating information and events to their interest areas. The foundation for assisting an autistic child is to know them, their interests, their likes and dislikes, and also what causes them anxiety.

CHAPTER 12

Joe Begins to Step Out of His Inner World

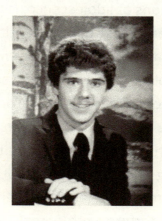

High School

A Whole New World

Life changed for us when Joe entered high school. He seemed to like it. He had different teachers for different subjects and did well with the daily changes. He actually woke up on time, even though he continued to stay awake until 2 a.m. I dropped him off at school in the morning, and he took the school bus home in the late afternoon. We attended sports games and other school events. I taught at a neighboring school so I was included in many teacher events held at the high school. This enabled me to become acquainted with my son's teachers on a professional level. The teachers accepted my son's differences as a mere blip in their daily lives. Joe still struggled academically, but he passed his courses and seemed to want to attend class. This was a whole new world for us, and we enjoyed it for the respite it provided.

Insights on High School Age

The age range for this time of life is 12-18. The focus is on a sense of self-identity, still learning through action and solving problems using trial and error. High school is often seen in the context of the trials and tribulations of adolescence. High school is a time of deep self-evaluation and sense of self-identity. This is when teens evaluate themselves and begin to decide what they will do with their lives and what place they will hold in society. This is a time for the development of self-identity—a process that is easier for some than for others.

Autistic teens may have difficulty evaluating their skills and interests and putting that information into realistic use. This often can be problematic for autistic teens if the hopes and dreams of parents interfere with a realistic evaluation of the needs, hopes, and dreams of the autistic teen. It is imperative that parents realize it is their responsibility to assist their autistic teens in evaluating themselves and not vice versa.

Changes in How Teens Think
Adolescence is a time of change whether one is autistic or not. The changes in the thinking process are the same in autistic teens as in non-autistic teens but the changes might be slower because they often require social interaction. Given that autistic teens have difficulty communicating with others, changes in the autistic teen's thinking process may be delayed.

In this stage of life, teens begin to develop a more adult level of thinking called abstract thinking. Abstract thinking aids in problem-solving, decision-making, and projecting consequences of events into the future. This abstract thinking also helps teens evaluate themselves for a sense of identity. For example, when a teen realizes that science and biology are major interests and enjoys helping others, he/she decides to become a doctor. That's a much more realistic decision compared to pursuing their dream as a five-year-old to become an astronaut because now the decision is based on actual skills and interests. Also, at this time, the teen begins to decide the kind of medicine he/she wants to practice and what the work will entail. Abstract thinking can help the teen decide whether being an ER doctor, surgeon, or family doctor is best. The teen can "see" into the future and imagine each lifestyle and work environment and if it is suited to them.

An Autistic Difference
Because the brain has difficulty functioning in an abstract thinking mode when the individual is in a state of anxiety, abstract thinking is problematic with autistic teens. Since this newfound way of thinking is not completely developed, teens usually seek out advice and assurance from their peers. Teens usually steer away from parental advice at this stage because parents, "don't understand." And honestly, parents usually don't understand due to the fact that the thought processes of parents are more advanced. This situation, of course, can cause tension between parents and teens. This is also true of autistic teens, who will gravitate toward others they believe may be more of an authority in certain areas than their parents.

Realistic vs. Idealistic
Interestingly, as teens become more realistic about themselves and what they may become in society, they also become more idealistic in their views of society as a whole. They see the possibilities that society can offer even as they also may become disillusioned and cynical. Many autistic teens, however, are wholly idealistic about society and world events because they have difficulty understanding human nature and how it might

undermine that scenario. They also tend to naively gravitate toward authority figures without realistically evaluating them.

Adolescence and high school can be tumultuous, to say the least, for teens and parents alike. Autistic teens also may have difficulty with self-evaluation due to their limited interests and experiences. The difficulty also may arise from lack of focus that does not allow self-evaluation to take place.

Social interaction, which is so important to teens, may be more difficult for autistic teens. Many autistic teens lack basic social skills like eye contact to enable them to develop close friendships. Also, some professionals believe that autistic teens never really develop abstract thinking so their ability to project consequences into the future is impaired, which affects their decision-making and problem-solving capacity. This may be true but I have some reservations. I believe that we, as parents, can help young children and autistic teens understand the consequences of their behavior. We just may need to be creative about how we do it.

Life with Joe: Achieving Identity

Joe's middle school principal, along with most of his teachers, agreed that Joe was incapable of attending a traditional high school. They told me that he should attend a special school in order to learn to work in a "sheltered workshop." Sheltered workshops are designed for disabled people who cannot work in other areas of society. The environment is "sheltered" in that it is developed and designed to meet the needs of those who are mentally and/or physically disabled or unable to work in mainstream society. The employees are sheltered or protected from types of environments in which they would not function well. The work in these workshops is similar to factory assembly lines.

I knew this was not the environment for Joe. I knew that he was too intelligent and too eager to learn to spend his life in a sheltered workshop, and I insisted that he attend a traditional high school. Even though money was tight, I opted to send Joe to a private high school that was significantly smaller than the neighboring public school. I believed that the smaller class size would be good for Joe, and he would receive more positive and individualized attention.

A Federal Law?

While Joe was still in middle school and I was attending college working on my degree, I had the opportunity to work with a fellow college student on the education requirements for children with special needs or disabilities. This fellow student, M., also had a son with special needs. Her son was close in age to Joe and needed special attention in school. He had cerebral palsy. M.'s son needed someone to assist him with walking, eating, and interpreting his verbal communication. M. had the heart and soul of an activist; the word "no" was not in her vocabulary, and she could not rest until all children had equal educational opportunities to reach their potential.

One day after class, she asked if I would join a roundtable discussion regarding the special education needs of children in school. At that time, there really was nothing substantial in schools to address the needs of children with disabilities. For the most part, our special needs children were considered society's discards. As parents, we saw the value of our children but rarely did anyone else see their value or potential. M. would not accept this. We were soul sisters.

M. gathered five mothers of children with disabilities and special needs in a room at the college and discussed our children's abilities and disabilities. We discussed the pros and cons of different types of educational programs and believed we came up with a realistic wish list for schools to implement including educating teachers and administrators about different types of disabilities, including cerebral palsy and autism. In fact, most of the mothers of children with special needs in this group either were teachers or studying to become teachers, so we knew what was needed when it came to our wish list.

Yes, a Federal Law!
M. applied and was accepted to be a member of a White House committee that was developing federal special education guidelines for public schools in the United States. She traveled to Washington, D.C. with our wish list in hand, and most of our wish list was included in the guidelines and became federal law. M. had been successful in pleading our case to the committee, and Public Law 94-142 paved the way for the present-day *Individuals with Disabilities Educational Act*, otherwise known as, *IDEA*.

The Needed Help
Our children and all children with special needs would receive the educational assistance they needed to develop their

potential. We had such high hopes but it took time for the law's provisions to be implemented. Our children did not significantly benefit from it but other children did. We were still very pleased with the outcome. It was with this in mind that I made the decision to have Joe attend a small private school. For the most part, it was a good decision. I was able to become acquainted with Joe's teachers and work with them to help him in his learning process. Some of his teachers tutored Joe either before or after school since Joe was better at focusing one-on-one.

Others Enter Joe's Life
As Joe grew older, I realized that other people needed to be a part of Joe's life. He needed to begin to become comfortable with the assistance of others besides me. He was growing up, and his world was getting larger. I wanted that for Joe. I did not want him to be imprisoned in a tiny albeit safe world. I truly wanted him to spread his wings. It began with others tutoring him. That meant, of course, the teachers would tutor him in their ways, not his. Still, I would go over subject material with him and relate it to maps and countries, and this helped as Joe progressed through the four years of high school. Joe was inching out of his own personal world. He began to speak in sentences. The sentences were related only to his *interest areas,* but they were sentences. He related stories of what teachers did or said in class. He wanted to go to sports events like football and basketball games held at the school. This was a very special time for me. Watching Joe step out of his world was exhilarating.

Vulnerability
I realized Joe was vulnerable, but I hoped that this school

environment would be safe for him. It was in some ways but not in other ways. Unfortunately, predators notice a vulnerable teen and take advantage, and one did take advantage of Joe, who was a young, vulnerable teen. He was abused by a counselor at his high school who was a member of a Catholic religious order. However, Joe's inner strength came to his rescue, and he did not wind up retreating back to his safe, isolated world.

Initially, the school administration denied any abuse. However, we filed a lawsuit that years later helped other victims of this counselor and eventually led to a change in the school's policies so that no other child would be victimized. My hope is that it continues to protect others in need.

Thinking of the Future

In high school, Joe began to think about how he fit into the world. Joe liked maps and initially wanted to be a cartographer until he realized being a cartographer required extensive study of subjects he didn't like such as math. He rethought his initial decision and realized he loved books even more than maps. Books were his favorite companions. They were his friends. They gave him information and took him on adventures to faraway places where he met new and interesting people. With that in mind, he decided that he would love to work in a library. This was good choice for Joe. He could spend the day surrounded by his beloved books. He cared for them, learned how to repair them, and learned how to help others find the books for which they were looking. He found his place in society there.

In his very quiet and unassuming manner, Joe proved many people wrong. He did not just get a certificate of attendance or need to work in a sheltered workshop. Just like elementary and middle school, Joe graduated with his high school diploma and the President's Academic Fitness Award. Never sell our autistic children short. They can create and achieve miracles. Just give them the helping hand they need. Helping our autistic children to realize what they are capable of doing, achieve at their own personal level, and realistically evaluate their abilities creates a motivated teenager with a drive to achieve. It is a partnership between parent and teen.

The Autistic Difference: **High School**
• *Ego Identity: Who Am I?---Erikson*

<u>Whose There to Help?</u>
Autistic adolescents experience the same misgivings regarding the ability of their parents to give advice about certain subjects and they, too, will turn to friends for advice. Autistic teens may not have the same quantity or variety of friends as non-autistic teens so choices in the decision-making process may be limited.

<u>Fitting In</u>
Given that autistic teens usually have difficulty in social situations, their desire to "fit in" also may be stronger than a non-autistic teen. They may perform behaviors at the request of "friends" because they want or need to be part of the group. In this way, autistic teens are more vulnerable than non-autistic teens. Subtle behavioral changes are important cues or red flags that may signal a problematic situation for an autistic teen.

<u>Stay Involved</u>
Since this high school stage heavily focuses on socialization and developing relationships outside the boundaries of family,

parents need to be as involved in as many aspects of the autistic teen's life as possible. There may be a fine line between being a "helicopter parent" and an involved parent. There is a difference. A helicopter parent tries to control aspects of the teen's life, including not only the teen but those who interact with the teen. An involved parent is observant and discusses situations, relationships, and events with the teen. An involved parent goes to activities as a spectator or as an assistant but not to control the teen.

More than parents of non-autistic children, parents of autistic teens stepping into the halls of high school benefit from observing subtle behavior changes in their teens, knowing their teen's friends, grades, and overall academics. Parents of autistic teens must be very aware of the level of anxiety the new high school situation presents to the teen such as new routines, new friendships, expectations, and responsibilities.

The Autistic Difference: High School
• *Concrete Activities: Needs-on activities to learn, trial-and-error problem-solving.*
• *Abstract thinking: consequences of decisions into future, drop back to Concrete Thinking when stressed, anxious or ill---Piaget.*

Adult Thinking
When considering teens and abstract thinking, many professionals believe that autistic teens are particularly incapable of thinking abstractly. I question this belief. Many autistic children and teens experience lifelong and sometimes debilitating anxiety. Because anxiety causes a reversion to concrete thinking, it happens to many autistic teens on a regular

basis. This does not mean the autistic teen is incapable of abstract thinking. Everyone, and I do mean everyone, falls back to concrete thinking when anxious or stressed. The brain cannot function well with logical, rational thinking and decision-making when emotions are high. This neurological fact. It is true of every human. When calm and not anxious, autistic teens can and often do experience the benefits of abstract thinking to project present behavior to future consequences.

Self-Evaluation

The average autistic teen may require more individual discussions with adults to self-evaluate and plan for the future. This need does not mean that the autistic teen is incapable of self-evaluation and life planning. Too often, autistic teens are labeled incapable when, in fact, they only require a little more consideration and assistance. If the high school faculty does not provide the extra assistance that the autistic teen needs, then the responsibility falls upon the shoulders of the parents. Because they know and understand their teens' abilities better than anyone, parents of autistic teens, in particular, should play a strong role in planning for the teen's future.

Reality

Parents/teachers need to consider their teen's interests and capabilities realistically so that the resulting plan for the future is realistic. Parents of autistic teens also need to be aware of the possibility that they might inadvertently influence their teen's life plan with their own personal desires. This is common with parents of all teens but especially with parents of autistic children because we want the best for our children, too.

Self-Esteem, Self-Worth---Cooley
This adolescent stage is the threshold of adulthood. It is our job as parents and teachers to help autistic teens realistically evaluate themselves including interests and abilities, skills, personalities, and temperaments of teens. We discuss who they are with them, not who we want them to be. We listen and truly hear their ideas and suggestions.

Needs Based Motivation---Maslow
Since autism affects social skills such as eye contact, autistic teens may shrink from developing social opportunities. Help them practice these skills with family members and friends. The objective is to help autistic teens develop sufficient social skills so that they may one day realize their academic and career goals.

Abilities Based Motivation---Bandura
As their abstract thinking develops, teens more often than not want the advice of other teens. It's important to try to understand their choices, decisions, and dreams in the context of their idealistic thinking processes. Adults need to try to see the world through the eyes of our teens for they are not yet developed to the extent they can see the world through our eyes.

CHAPTER 13

Joe Goes Against All Odds

College Experience/Young Adult

Events of a Lifetime

This is the stage in Joe's life that I will never forget: He went to college going *against all odds*. It was something that was not supposed to happen but it did. He was finally accepted for the brilliant person that he is. His college professors were astonished at his ability to remember facts. When he became assistant to the dean, he earned the respect of the other college students. In his sophomore year, he won the Trivial Pursuit championship. He finally found the environment where he could shine and bloom into the adult he was meant to be. The hopes and dreams that I held so close in my heart for him were finally coming true.

Insights on Young Adulthood

Young Adulthood includes ages 18-40 and focuses on developing intimate, long-term relationships, develop abstract thinking and understanding future consequences of present behavior.

Young adulthood is the first step into the full-fledged world of adulthood. The emphasis is not only on developing long-term relationships but also on developing oneself for career and family.

Abstract thinking is vitally important in this stage because young adults are making decisions that will affect them for the rest of their lives. The more time, energy, and thought that goes into the decision-making process, the less time they will spend later in life repairing mistakes.

Because young adults have the tendency to want to get settled in life as quickly as possible, it is advantageous for parents and friends to discuss long-term decisions with them. Our young autistic adults, especially if they experience stress and anxiety, may not be aware of long-term consequences of their actions.

Life with Joe: Achieving Long-Term Relationships
Joe's life to this point consistently proved the professionals wrong. Joe received his elementary and middle school diplomas. Though the experience was very difficult for him, Joe did learn the material and was able to test high enough to graduate. Against the advice of teachers and principals, I enrolled Joe in a high school noted for its college prep program.

Though this experience was again difficult, Joe completed the high school academic material with scores high enough to not only receive his high school diploma but also to receive the

President's Academic Fitness Award! Joe proved the professionals wrong again!

The problem was that the professionals who advised me did not know enough about autism and definitely did not know Joe. I knew Joe. I lived with Joe. I paid attention to him and his interests. I tutored him in all of his subject courses. I knew how he learned. I knew how brilliant he was. The professionals saw him for short periods of time. Teachers worked with him in groups of 30 or more students, which is an environment where Joe shuts down, while other professionals believed he was incapable of learning or being a productive part of society.

One of a Kind

The idea that "one label fits all" was unacceptable to me. My belief is that each and every child is an individual, whether disabled or not, and needs to be considered for who he/she is. I truly know how difficult it is working with and getting to know children individually. I have been in the field of education for over 40 years. I have been a teacher (K-12), a high school counselor, a school psychologist, and now a college instructor. I know the time it takes to get to know students one-on-one. It is imperative that teachers truly listen to parents because parents know their children better than anyone else. It is a wise educational professional who truly takes into consideration what parents say about their children and themselves.

Decisions to be Made

When I helped Joe apply to college, we only considered small private colleges where class sizes would be manageable for him. Joe and I discussed the many wonderful courses he could take, including several in his interest areas of geography and history. Joe was considering the prospect of attending college and studying his favorite topics with a little anxiety but also with much anticipation. He was pleased when he received a call to come to one of his chosen colleges for an acceptance interview. I went with Joe to the interview because I was his advocate. I am so glad that I did. It was quite an experience for a mother, so used to hopeless negativity from educators, to see the reaction of the dean of the geography department to Joe, my incredible and autistic son.

The Interview
The interview started out pleasantly and just got better as it proceeded. The dean asked Joe questions about geography, maps, countries, borders, and country name changes. Joe, of course, knew every answer. To say the dean was dazzled would be an understatement. I thought the dean would pop right out of his chair in glee. He smiled, laughed, and thoroughly enjoyed himself. It seemed that the dean and Joe became fast friends, right there in front of my eyes. The dean looked at Joe with pride and astonishment. I was sure by his reaction to Joe that he did not see brilliant, autistic potential students every day.
I had not previously told the dean or anyone else about Joe's autism. Nor were there any special needs programs in colleges at the time. Nevertheless, Joe shined. It was his day. A short time into the interview, the dean told Joe that he was accepted as a freshman. Joe beamed. And so did the dean. It took many years, but it happened: Someone else besides me knew that Joe was brilliant. The dean shook Joe's hand as he welcomed him to the college. I knew this moment was worth every minute of struggle

Joe and I shared throughout the years. For the first time in his life, Joe was accepted and actually celebrated for being himself.

The Initial College Experience

College was a big step for Joe and me. He would be away from home all week staying in the college dorm. Joe would need to make decisions on his own without me to assist and support him. He would need to work with his professors without my assistance. He was eager to begin a new life. However, he wanted to do so slowly. For the first two months of college, Joe came home every weekend. That was fine with me, but I really did want him to experience some social life in college. I wanted Joe to make friends.

One day, I discovered that there would be a football game and concert on campus on a Saturday. I thought Joe would enjoy these activities since we had attended them when Joe was in high school. Joe declined. Eventually, he agreed to go to a Saturday night play and loved the experience so much he did not want to come home on weekends again. It almost was a struggle to get him to come home for holidays. Joe was learning that life could be fun. He wanted to make friends. I am not sure whether it was that Joe changed or that he had finally found an environment that could accept his differences as positive.

Joe enjoyed his classes and was able to focus better because almost every course he took aligned with one of his interests. He could discuss the information, taking an active part in the class. He not only fit in, he also shined. Joe knew the subject matter and could discuss it, and the only problem was that he still had difficulty writing essays for assignments and projects so he used a tutor. The one-on-one work enabled him to write.

A Step Forward

The intake dean happened to teach one of Joe's courses and got to know Joe better. The dean was astonished by the breadth of Joe's knowledge in geography and history. By the end of the first school year, Joe was called into that dean's office and was offered a work study position. He accepted and became the dean's academic assistant. Talk about being accepted: Joe had just hit a home run. He had the time of his life.

Joe was busy with campus activities and tutoring international students in geography and history. He began to attend the weekly study groups held in the dean's home. He loved these meetings because they were small and only included students who were very serious about the topics.

Joe was enjoying himself like never before. He made friends, some of whom are still friends today, decades later. The relationships Joe developed with his professors somewhat replaced his lost father relationship.

I think Joe felt affirmed as a person when he was accepted by his professors as someone of value - valuable enough to become academic assistant to the dean.

Joe also began attending an Al-Anon group. It took years but he finally accepted his inability to have a relationship with his father. He now helps people in similar situations to attend groups and shares with them how it has helped him.

My Going Forward

By this time, I was working as a high school counselor, and I loved my job working with at-risk teens, putting my experiences with Joe to good use. I also helped develop a special education department at the high school to assist students with learning disabilities that had not yet been identified. After a few years in this position, the high school principal informed the staff that the school might close. It was to be integrated with another neighboring high school. Many of us were being laid off and since I was the counselor with least seniority, I was to be let go.

What Do I Do Now?
I began the hunt for another job, but positions were few and far between, and schools were not hiring. A few years earlier, a family member moved with her family to Southern California where they were doing well. Jobs seemed to be booming in California, and I had always wanted to visit. I not so secretly wanted to move there. I wanted to be warm. Though I loved Chicago, its winters could be brutal. I would get pictures of family members in California barbequing outside at Christmas and swimming in the pool on New Year's Day. I thought a visit was in order. What did I have to lose?

My fiancé John, Joe, and I took a week-long trip to Southern California in late June. We took Amtrak and thoroughly enjoyed the experience. Joe loved the train ride as it let him see the country, a dream of his since he was six years old. When we got off the train in Los Angeles, blue skies and bright sunlight greeted us. We drove from Los Angeles to San Diego along the coast. I loved everything about Southern California. I felt at home.

A Big Step
At the end of the next school year, I resigned my job, and Joe and I moved to California. John came out a few months later after completing his Chicago area teaching contract. I mention this move because it had such an impact on Joe. In Chicago, Joe had

finally found an environment that he loved and that accepted him as a valued person. He hated the idea of moving and leaving his newfound wonderful world. I truly understood his feelings. But I was in a state of emotional turmoil. I had been the sole support for us for many years. I needed to make sure Joe and I had a roof over our heads and food in our mouths. I lucked out and received grants and scholarships for Joe's college tuition but it did not pay for all the costs. I needed to have a steady job and Illinois could not provide that. I was frightened I could be homeless if I could not find a job.

Even though taking Joe from his beloved environment would be difficult, I knew it was the only way to support us. If I did not have a job, Joe would not be able to attend the college, anyway. Either way, Joe's dream would end. I was between a rock and a hard place. I did the only thing that I could think to help Joe. I offered to have Joe stay in Illinois and live with his grandmother and fly him to California for holidays. Joe declined. He did not want to be left alone. For better or worse, we packed the car and started on our journey to a new chapter of our lives in California.

On Our Way

The trip was difficult for all of us; we knew life was changing but did not actually know what to expect. Joe was missing his college friends, and I was anxious about finding a job and leaving John behind for the next eight months. John, too, was stressed since Joe and I were moving and temporarily leaving him behind. That first summer in California was difficult. Joe was depressed and very unhappy. He was quiet and refused to do much at all. He missed his friends. I was sad for Joe. I hated to see my child so unhappy. Shortly after we arrived in California, Joe and I visited a sister school to the one he had attended in Illinois. The geography dean from Illinois gave Joe the name of a professor with whom he felt Joe should discuss a transfer. The dean in Illinois thought Joe was a special student and wanted to help him adjust. Before classes started for the semester, Joe met with this new professor, who happened to be the dean of the history department. Joe liked him at the first meeting. They seemed to click. Joe was beginning to feel a little better about this school environment. The school was new, the grounds beautiful. And, best of all, the new history dean reminded Joe of his former geography dean.

Joe Adjusting

As Joe took required courses, he got to know some professors and other students. The history department dean also got to know Joe, and at the end of the first semester, Joe was offered a job as the dean's academic assistant. It took a few months but Joe was picking up his life. He again started to attend sports events, campus activities, and concerts. He still needed some tutoring but for the majority of his courses, he paid attention and was able to focus better and complete the required work. Ultimately, Joe had experiences at the California college that he could never have had in Illinois.

Joe joined a group that traveled to Mexico every month and volunteered at an orphanage. They played with the children. They painted walls. They repaired what had been broken. Joe learned to become more social. His world again was expanding. He loved going to Mexico each month as it was an extension of his interest in geography and history. He was beginning to live a dream he had as a child to travel and have adventures, not just in books but in real life. This Mexico group also visited a place called the "garbage dump" where homeless people lived. The group delivered food, clothing, toiletries, and other necessities. In high school, Joe often had visited homeless shelters with a volunteer program that the students were encouraged to join. With this Mexico group, he was doing familiar activities. He looked forward to the adventure every month. Joe enjoyed the bus rides there and back and being with the other college students, all of which helped him with socialization.

The Trip of a Lifetime
In Joe's last year of college, his dean developed a study abroad program. The main site would be the University of Mexico City, but the study program would include travel to various parts of Mexico from cities to jungles and the Yucatan. The dean asked me if Joe could go on this trip. I was stunned. It never occurred to me that Joe would have the opportunity to experience something like that. The dean told me he thought the experience would be good for Joe. He believed it would help Joe with his socialization. I agreed. The only problem was the fee. It was an expensive trip. John and I had just married and were establishing ourselves in jobs. Money was tight. John and I discussed this with Joe, who badly wanted to go on the trip. Talk about an adventure. This was it. John and I could not break his heart. I contacted Joe's grandmother and we decided to divide the fees between her, John, and I. John took on extra jobs at school, and I worked extra hours. We miraculously came up with the entire amount. This is the point when Joe's grandmother fell in love with John. I asked why she cared so much for him, and she replied, "He's taking care of my grandson." That was all that was needed to be said.

Living His Dream

Joe left on his 16-week study abroad trip in his last year of college. I had never seen him happier. He was embarking on a lifelong dream to lands unknown. He was so excited he could barely sleep the night before he left. I went to campus with him the morning of his flight to Mexico City. He met his dean and the other student travelers, they rode together from the college campus to LAX. I waved to him as he started the first step in his adventure of a lifetime. I felt the same way I had felt on Joe's first day of kindergarten: I was filled with hope, anxiety, and pride. An adventure of a lifetime was exactly what the trip turned out to be.

He loved every minute of it. He visited a wide variety of Mexican cities. He went to small towns and participated in traditional events, and he used a machete to cut his path through the Mexican jungle on his way to the Yucatan. He studied the Spanish language, something he had done in high school, and the Mexican and Aztec cultures. He visited and climbed the pyramids. He had the time of his life. This experience was what Joe needed to develop his social skills. Joe was growing up.

During that study abroad program, Joe took a side trip to Guatemala on a bus with a few other students. On the journey, the bus was stopped by army soldiers who took some passengers off the bus and handcuffed them. Joe was not questioned by the soldiers and neither were the other students with him. Quite an experience, but he took it in stride. He was in a foreign country and, through his readings, he knew things like this happened in Central American countries. Joe loved Guatemala for its colorful houses and friendly people. He loved this side trip. Talk about an adventure! When the trip ended, Joe was a different person.

He was more confident. After all, he had forged his way through the jungle with a machete. He could do anything.

You Want Me to do What?
Shortly after returning from the trip, the dean contacted me. He said he had a class to fill and needed a teacher. He asked me to come in to talk about it. I did, though I wondered why he wanted to talk to me. The dean explained the course to me. It sounded interesting and after a few minutes, the dean told me when the course would start and handed me a textbook. I was confused. He said, "You have the job." I told him he did not have my resume or letters of recommendation, nothing. How could he know I would be able to teach this course, and teach it well? How could he be sure I was qualified? He looked at me and said something that I will never forget, "You are Joe's mom. That is all the recommendation I need." I taught at that college for 12 years. I loved the experience. Joe graduated with a bachelor's degree in history and a minor in geography. Since I was a faculty member, I was able to walk down the aisle with the other faculty members and the graduating class. It was an experience of a lifetime for me. It was something I never thought would or could possibly happen and I will never forget it.

The Autistic Difference: Young Adulthood
• *Intimacy: Developing Relationships---Erikson*

<u>Friendships</u>
The is desire for long-term relationships is the same for autistic young adults. They, too, want a sense of intimacy with others. However, this sense of intimacy may be more difficult and take longer to achieve. Since many autistic young adults have issues

with social behavior such as eye contact and speaking with others, the development of intimate relationships can require intense focus and motivation.

What Can I Do?
The autistic young adult can join clubs in college and attend events such as sports and concerts. Any of these types of activities will lend themselves to meeting people with similar interests. Tutoring in an area of interest is also a good way to develop social skills. Since many autistic young adults are good with technology, tutoring or assisting others with technology also is a way to meet people. These examples may not in and of themselves lead an autistic young adult to find friends, but they are ways in which autistic young adults can learn and practice social skills to be used later in developing friendships. Everything is a process. What might come easily for non-autistic young adults might be difficult and exhausting for an autistic young adult. Practicing social skills is imperative for autistic young adults to achieve a sense of intimacy and develop long-term relationships.

As awareness of autism grows, people are becoming more tolerant and comfortable with autistic children and adults. Autistic young adults may find it easier to develop relationships as this trend continues.

The Autistic Difference: Young Adulthood
• *Concrete Thinking: Need hands-on activities to learn, trial-and-error problem-solving.*
•*Abstract thinking: project consequences of decisions into future, back to Concrete Thinking when stressed, anxious or ill---Piaget*

Adult Thinking Again

Although many professionals believe that it is not possible for autistic young adults to develop abstract thinking, I believe it's possible. Unlike other professionals, I have a different take on the development of abstract thinking in autistic young adults. I believe that most autistic young adults tend to fall back into concrete thinking more often than non-autistic young adults who do not experience the same level or frequency of anxiety.

Autistic young adults also may be more vulnerable to suggestions made by someone they perceive as an authority figure, whether they really are or not. This occurs because autistic young adults are anxious and look for people, belief systems, and philosophies that will help them to feel less anxious. Medication can help but it does not completely relieve the vulnerability experienced by autistic young adults.

Discussions and involvement in the life of the autistic young adult can go a long way to counter some of the negative aspects of vulnerability. This is a good time to discuss "who" might be considered an authority and "why" these authorities can be trusted. This is a difficult discussion if someone who was considered to be a trustworthy authority figure proved to be untrustworthy. It is good to make it clear that if the autistic young adult is ever uncomfortable with someone's suggestions, they should discuss the matter with parents and other trusted resources. These are ways to assist autistic young adults to practice abstract thinking that helps their development and growth.

The following points are true for those who choose to go to college and those who choose not to do so. Encouragement, acceptance, and assistance are the components of success.

Self-Esteem, Self-Worth---Cooley

Colleges now have special needs departments that give students assistance to help them succeed in college. These departments inform the teachers that a particular student requires special assistance, which may include notetakers and special provisions for testing. Success builds self-esteem and self-worth.

Needs Based Motivation---Maslow

For autistic college students, the hierarchy of needs is in full bloom especially is they are away from home. Eating, sleeping well, feeling, being safe, belonging to groups, and succeeding are all in play. Discussing each area for possible solutions to problems that may arise helps that problems will not arise.

Abilities Based Motivation---Bandura

Registration with the college's special needs department helps students be as successful as possible. Suggesting tutoring when needed and making that option acceptable helps to ensure success. Encouragement and acceptance motivates a college student to continue and ultimately succeed.

CHAPTER 14

Joe Goes Against All Odds Again

Adulthood/Graduate School

Getting His Wings

Young adulthood is when Joe began to think independently. He was becoming his own person. He chose when and where he would volunteer. He chose his friends and began to socialize often. He was finding his wings and starting to fly on his own. It is exactly what parents want for their child; however worrisome it might be.

Not everyone wants to go to graduate school, especially because it is time consuming and expensive. However, it is necessary for many professions. In this stage, older young adults focus on developing long-term relationships and career choices. It is a time when decision-making has long-term and perhaps permanent consequences.

Life with Joe: Achieving Long-Term Relationships

After graduating from college with a bachelor's degree in history and a minor in geography, Joe needed to reinvent himself. He was no longer a student. He was a college graduate, an adult. College was a unique and wonderful experience for Joe, but now he needed to decide on what else he was going to do. This is not easy for an autistic adult. Even though Joe developed socially in college, it was a protected environment.

Another Round of Decision-Making

Joe felt lost at the prospect of leaving his campus. He wanted to stay there forever. Since Joe enjoyed tutoring international students and was good at it, he explored teaching as a profession. Joe applied and was accepted into his college's teacher credentialing program. It allowed him to stay on campus for another year while taking the required courses. However, Joe quickly realized the courses in this field were not in his interest area, and he struggled a great deal. He dropped out of the program after realizing that being an elementary or middle school teacher would not be an ideal career for him. We reevaluated. Joe's forte was in remembering vast amounts of knowledge and sharing this knowledge with others one-on-one or in a very small group. We considered tutoring and found an organization that specialized in teaching ESL, English as a second language to immigrants. We found out that the class sizes were small and the organization supplied the teacher materials. Joe applied for a teaching position and was quickly accepted. Joe had been doing well teaching ESL. It seemed that the clients liked him, especially the young women in his class. They would bring Joe homemade food such as tacos and tamales, which he quickly devoured. This encouraged the young women to bring even more food, which made Joe very happy indeed. He was a perfect match for this job so it was really sad when the organization needed to close its doors.

That opportunity had been perfect for Joe. It was our hope that Joe would find a permanent place to work but that seemed to elude him. He again had to redefine himself. Joe was a little at odds with himself. It was difficult for him to know what to do next. We sat down many times and discussed what he would enjoy. I knew discussing options and helping Joe was a must. Whatever Joe would do needed to be in one of his interest areas or he would not function.

In our discussions, because of his varied experiences, the idea of service work came up until he could find another job. Joe had spent years volunteering in homeless shelters and in Mexico. He had spent years in college volunteering as a tutor for international students and loved being with people from other countries. We investigated the Catholic Worker, a homeless shelter in Santa Ana. There were some people at his church who volunteered there and praised the experience. The agency was housed in a large building in an area that allowed it to easily service the poor and homeless. Joe immediately liked what he saw. He liked the friendly staff and the people who came for meals. Joe began volunteering there a couple of times a week. We spent time there as a family on holidays, and our family became friends with the staff. Joe became more involved with the shelter. After about a year, Joe decided to become part of the full-time staff. His job required him to live on the premises with the other full-time staff members. In exchange, he received room and board and a small stipend. He was eager to begin. He packed his clothes, and off he went on his new adventure, loving every minute of it.

Joe's Life as a Helper

Joe was able to sit with the homeless people and discuss various topics, which also included discussions of world events. Oh, he loved doing this. He listened to their life stories and because Joe was so nonjudgmental, people opened up to him and related to him many of the problems that caused them to become homeless. Many people told him that alcohol and drugs were the main reasons. Many others had mental illnesses that made it difficult for them to remain employed. A large number of homeless men were military veterans suffering from PTSD, post traumatic stress disorder. They, too, needed to talk. Joe was the perfect person, a good listener.

Every morning after helping to serve breakfast and cleaning up, he sat with various people over coffee and listened to them talk about their problems, their hopes and dreams. Joe was good at listening and remembering what he heard. This talent helped him with homeless people who wanted to be heard. Joe developed an uncanny ability to pinpoint the core of a problem. It was like he was able to find a needle in a haystack and pull it out to show the world. This is what he did with homeless people. They related their life stories and he listened. Then, out of the blue, he would make a comment that pinpointed the core issue of their problems. It was amazing. Joe had done this with me several times so I knew how amazing it was to hear him get to the heart of an issue as easily as ordering a pizza. Once he did, it was difficult not to see it and acknowledge it. He always stated it in such a matter-of-fact manner that it was impossible to deny. It was one of his gifts.

At the Fair

One bright and sunny afternoon, John, Joe, and I along with a friend visiting from Chicago went to the county fair where we met a man who ran up to Joe and threw his arms around him. The man wore a county fair security uniform and hugged Joe like an old friend. He asked Joe how he was and then introduced himself to the rest of us. He explained that he knew Joe from the homeless shelter.

He looked fondly at Joe and told us Joe was a good listener. He told us what he experienced when he was homeless and jobless. He said that he and Joe spoke every morning over coffee. Because of his talks with Joe, he was able to stop drinking and start attending Alcoholics Anonymous. He became sober and found a job. After working for a while, he met a woman, they dated, married, and had a child.

This man hugged me and thanked me for Joe. He told me Joe had saved his life. Because of his morning talks with Joe, he was able to have a life. As he left, he turned, pointed to Joe and said, "Joe, don't ever forget that you saved a life, my life." Well, by that time, I was a heap of mush, John was smiling, and Elaine was in tears. Joe, of course, took it in stride, but I could tell he was beaming. This was Joe: quiet, a good listener, insightful, a natural helper.

Graduate School?

While staying at the homeless shelter, Joe had the opportunity to meet a wide variety of people. The volunteers came from all walks of life. There were former pimps and ex-prostitutes. There were doctors, lawyers, and college professors. Joe spent time with all of them. One, in particular, was a professor of political science at a local university. One day as Joe and the professor were talking, the professor mentioned Joe might like to go to graduate school and study political science, which had become one of Joe's interests. While working at the homeless shelter, Joe also worked as a campaign volunteer. The professor told Joe it would be a good idea to apply to graduate school. Joe and I discussed it, he decided to apply. He was accepted and was able to receive a state financial needs grant to help with the tuition. Graduate school was, of course, a struggle as Joe still had difficulty completing written assignments and organizing thoughts on paper but he did most of the course work on his own. He had some help from the college professor he met at the homeless shelter. Although Joe loved learning the subject matter, school was such a struggle that he considered dropping out. He liked reading books and he loved learning. He was studying subjects that really interested him. Joe always had the ability to absorb information and retain it, but he had difficulty expressing in written form and in his own words what he learned. Still, academic work was familiar to him and Joe did his best. He got good grades - mostly Bs, some As. We were all pleased.

A Thesis? Yes, a Thesis!
Then came the dreaded event: Writing his master's thesis, the culmination of the master's program. It took Joe a while to decide on a topic but he finally did: "The Drug War." (Society's struggle with illegal drugs.) Joe was always good at research, reading, and absorbing information. Writing the thesis would be a different story. In doing his research, Joe discovered the writing of a local

county superior court judge who believed the *Drug War* caused more harm than good. This was what Joe thought, too. He planned to contact the judge for an interview and my first thought was, "Good luck." Judges are busy people and usually have no time for student interviews. But Joe called for an interview and was able to speak with the judge himself. They set a day and time for an interview. Joe acted like it was no big deal. Joe spent longer than planned with the judge. The judge was impressed with his knowledge of the situation and fascinated with his ideas. The judge spoke at length about his own ideas on ending the Drug War. At the end of the interview, the judge told Joe to contact him if he had further questions and that he was happy to help Joe with his thesis. And the judge was good to his word. The judge took all of Joe's subsequent calls and answered all of his questions. His only request was to have a copy of the thesis when it was completed.

Joe's nemesis was the organized writing of learned information. It was all but impossible for him. However, he never gave up. We finally came up with a way around it. He spoke his ideas into a tape recorder and we had the tapes transcribed by another student. Joe then met with his thesis adviser, the professor he met at the homeless shelter. His professor was impressed Joe had interviewed the judge. The professor was so pleased that he spent time with Joe organizing the thesis into sections for development. The rest is history.

Joe, happy to have two prominent people helping him, was eager to complete his thesis. The professor helped Joe with some revisions and the judge read it over for accuracy. It was finished. Joe received his master's degree in a wonderful ceremony with all of his homeless shelter friends in attendance. They even had a graduation party at the shelter. It was a great time for Joe. He had worked hard and achieved his dream of completing his master's degree. A few months later, a friend of ours read Joe's thesis and loved it. She asked for Joe's permission to use the thesis as a textbook for one of the college courses that she taught. Of course, he said yes.

Settling Into Life
Life was good for Joe at this time. He had his work at the homeless shelter. He kept in touch with his professor for several years, and he became good friends with the judge. A few years later, the judge ran for political office. He contacted Joe and asked if he would like to work on his campaign. Joe agreed and became a valued part of the campaign. Joe, with his special talent for maps, was in charge of mapping district information. When I visited the campaign office, people told me that they wouldn't know what to do without Joe. They showed me what his job position entailed. All of his interests culminated in this job: Maps, politics, history. He worked hard all his life with so many struggles. All of that was now behind him. He was working with a superior court judge, members of the judge's staff, and campaign volunteers, and the only thing he heard was praise for his special talents. Joe was needed for just being Joe. Isn't that all a mother wants for her child?

The Autistic Difference: *Adulthood*
• *Generativity: Helping Others---Erikson*

What Now?
This an important transition period for autistic young adults. Decisions regarding graduate school or career choices can be

stressful at this later stage. Due to the fact that graduate schools may not have the same academic support for special needs students as undergraduate programs, the experience can be daunting for an autistic adult. Graduate schools typically assign advisors to graduate students on a fairly random basis. The advisors may not have any expertise in assisting graduate students with particular learning needs. It may be necessary for the autistic adult entering graduate school to have a mentor who is aware of his/her needs and can assist with the graduate school process. This may not be an easy task to accomplish.

Career Choices
Autistic young adults at this later stage of development who choose to enter the workforce and take a job position may face similar difficulties. Since they have problems with socialization, they may be passed over for job promotions. Career advancement may be problematic for anyone with lesser social skills ability since job promotions often rely on social networking and interaction. However, with the rise of technology, there are job positions that may not require an abundance of social skills. As a matter of fact, many technology positions require the exact characteristics that are hallmarks of autism—for example, a capacity for intense focus.

The Autistic Difference: Adulthood
• *Concrete Thinking: Need hands-on activities to learn, trial-and-error problem-solving.*
•*Abstract Thinking: Project consequences of decisions into future, drop back to Concrete Thinking when stressed, anxious or ill---Piaget.*

I Do Know
The improvement of abstract thinking in autistic young adults is similar at this later stage. However, as previously mentioned, autistic adults still experience anxiety, which can hamper their consistent use of abstract thinking and their ability to make decisions based on present behavior and to project future consequences.

Anxiety
Anxiety is an ongoing characteristic of autism, which is understandable given the difficulty they experience attempting to fit into society and developing social skills. If the autistic child or adult is more comfortable in their own inner worlds, excursions into the outside world can be very anxiety-producing. More anxiety results in less consistent abstract thinking. Th is gap in abstract thinking can lead to a lack of good decisions or, unfortunately, a vulnerability to others who may not have the best interests of the autistic adult in mind.

Decisions, Decisions
Again, discussions that help the autistic adult consider elements of decision-making are helpful so that they know they have an available support system. The need that autistic individuals have for interaction with loved ones never seems to diminish. Instead, it seems to be constant and just changes in kind and intensity depending on their age and situation. Given that the autistic young adult in the later stage has inconsistent abstract thinking skills, parental or family support is imperative for their continued growth and development.

Self-Esteem, Self-Worth---Cooley

In this adult stage parent and teacher involvement is usually minimal. However, that minimal involvement needs to be weighed against what the autistic adult needs to fulfill their potential at this stage. Finding appropriate advocates is especially important at this stage of an autistic adult's life.

Needs Based Motivation---Maslow

It is important to evaluate the needs of the autistic adult at this stage in light of their goals. It can be a mountain of work, but it is incredibly worthwhile to assist and support an autistic adult in achieving his/her goals. This involvement relates love and caring to the autistic adult along with a sense of safety.

Abilities Based Motivation---Bandura

Helping adult autistic children to find an employment environment in which they can thrive is all important. Young adults spend a great deal of time at their place of employment, and they need to be comfortable and not overwhelmed in that environment. Discussing the different careers and employment environments is key.

CHAPTER 15

Joe Steps Out on His Own

Middle Adulthood

The Empty Nest

Oh, the empty nest. How could I deal with Joe moving out of our home and moving out with glee? He was looking forward to being on his own. He was 30 years old and wanted his own apartment. He received assistance from the housing authority so he could afford rent. The excitement of receiving furniture and household items from friends was almost more than he could bear. He roomed with another autistic young adult for two years before Joe took the initiative and found a more suitable apartment for himself. He enjoys living in that apartment to this day.

Insights on Adulthood

Adulthood includes ages 40-65 and focuses on care for future generations, continuing the development of abstract thinking, and understanding the consequences of present behaviors on the future. This is a time when the previous developmental stages culminate in a career and professional activities. It also is a time to develop family life, including marriage and rearing children. Autistic adults may or may not choose to marry and raise children, and they may have full or part-time jobs. It really depends on their level of autism and ability to function, and these decisions are important for both the autistic individual and his/her family to discuss together.

Life with Joe: Achieving Independence
While he worked at the homeless shelter, Joe and I spoke on the phone a few times a week. I needed the connection to him and to know that he was doing well. I was being a mom. One day, he sounded congested. I asked him how he felt, and he said he had the flu. I asked if he had talked to a doctor, and he told me that another member of the staff who was studying to be a nurse looked in on him. He said he was OK. He did not sound OK, but I trusted that the staff would take care of him.

The next day, I called again to see how he was doing, and he sounded worse than the day before. John and I drove over to see how he was really doing. When we arrived and went up to his room, we saw him lying in bed, sweating and bleary-eyed. I looked for a thermometer and took his temperature. It was almost 103. The building was old and drafty so Joe agreed to come home until he was better. We gathered Joe's things, brought him home, and nursed him back to health.

Not Just the Flu
However, the flu lasted much longer than it really should have. He seemed short of breath and was always tired. Joe was never the most energetic person, but now he was like a rag doll. A trip to the doctor would fix him up, I thought, and I made an

appointment. During the appointment, the doctor noticed a strange sound in Joe's chest and after some tests, she gave Joe medication and said to come back in a few days.

At the second appointment, she gave Joe another EKG. The results were the same. Something abnormal was going on. The doctor recommended Joe see a cardiologist. At the cardiologist's office the next week, Joe underwent several tests. The results that came back were shocking. Joe had an enlarged heart, a bundle branch blockage, and cardiomyopathy among other things. His heart function was down to 27% - just two percentage points from needing a heart transplant. He needed complete rest and specialized heart medication.

The flu had settled in his heart and caused some severe damage. He could no longer be in an environment where there was a greater possibility of being exposed to bacteria and viruses. His days at the homeless shelter as a staff member were over.

Recovering Brings Change
With rest and medication, Joe got better. However, the heart damage was permanent. About three years later, his heart function had increased slightly to 30%. Joe was feeling better and again needed to begin the task of redefining himself... Since Joe could no longer work at the homeless shelter, he needed to consider other options.

His soul searching again centered around his love of books. Working in the quiet environment of a library might be just the thing. A friend of ours knew the head librarian at the city library. We put together a resume and submitted it with the application; Joe was called in for an interview. The interview went well and Joe was hired. Joe loved the job, and the library staff seemed to love his work. He shelved books and learned to repair book spines, and he assisted library patrons in researching topics and finding appropriate books. He worked there for almost a year before he again became ill. The doctor believed that working five days a week was too much for Joe's heart and wrote a letter to the Social Security Administration office and the head librarian. Joe was given a volunteer job at the library so he could go in when he felt well enough to work. On the other days, he rested - a new requirement for him.

After a year or so, Joe visited the library at his former college where he had earned his bachelor's degree. After he explained his experience at the city library, the head librarian eagerly asked Joe to join the volunteer staff. He loved this position. He learned their method of caring for books, repairing them, and cleaning them. He shelved books and helped students research topics. He was again able to attend campus activities and events as a staff member, and he audited courses and discussed issues with the professors. He was in heaven.

Making Friends

Joe developed many relationships at this time, including some lasting friendships. At this time, Mike, one of his friends from their college in Illinois, moved to California to be near Joe. Mike had no family members left, and was all alone in the world. He had kept in touch with Joe all of these years and decided he would join Joe and our family in sunny, Southern California. This was good for Joe as he now had old friends and new friends. Joe introduced his old friends to his new friends creating a larger circle of friends - a wonderful, important goal for autistic adults.

Joe's Own Place

As Joe started to feel better, he again became restless with living at home. He noticed that all of his cousins were living on their own and most of them were married. Joe started to talk about having his own apartment. I did not know if this was possible but, as always, I was a willing supporter. I contacted the nonprofit Regional Center of Orange County in Santa Ana, California, which assisted Joe in many aspects of his life. Staff there told me about independent living programs for autistic adults and we applied for a *Section 8 housing voucher* for Joe to help with rental expenses. We also had applied and received Social Security disability for Joe. Finally, between his disability pay and the housing voucher, he was able to look for an apartment.

Through a socialization program at the Regional Center of Orange County, we met other families with autistic adults who wanted to live independently. We also met with several other families to find possible roommates for Joe. The roommate options were people with varied conditions such as mild to moderate autism, high-functioning Down's Syndrome and high-functioning intellectual disabilities. We wanted to find a compatible roommate for Joe - someone who was quiet, liked to read, and loved technology. We met with some parents for dinner and others for coffee and dessert. Joe chose one fellow that he would like as a roommate. He also was autistic and loved technology as much as Joe did. The young man agreed that he also would like to be Joe's roommate. Our two families searched for apartments, and we found a two-bedroom/two-bath apartment not far from our homes. It was near a shopping center and bus line so it seemed to be a perfect place.

Be Aware

An independent living organization referred to us by the Regional Center assisted Joe and his roommate with things they needed to do to live independently. For the most part, the situation was a good experience. Some of the workers were excellent, assisting with compassion and expertise. However, some of the workers were pretty awful and avoided performing activities that would assist Joe in his daily functioning. They spent their time with Joe reading or watching TV.

There was even verbal abuse that continued for several months before it was discovered, given Joe's inability to explain situations well. The abusive worker told Joe that he was not sick but lazy. This same worker would drop Joe off at a doctor's office and force him to walk to a bus stop in the heat in order to return home. Joe was in the third stage of congestive heart failure, and this behavior could have caused Joe to slide into the fourth and final stage. Such difficulties with communication and social interaction put our autistic adults especially at risk of abuse.

A Needed Change

Unfortunately, Joe's roommate was not as organized as Joe and tended to have problems with personal hygiene and cleanliness in the apartment. After two years, the stress and anxiety of having this roommate caused Joe to again become ill. We applied for a change in the voucher to a single rather than a two-bedroom apartment. Then we started apartment hunting again. This time, Joe took most of the responsibility for researching as he was determined to have the best environment possible. He found an apartment near his former college so he easily could get to his volunteer campus library job. Joe moved into his one-bedroom/one-bath apartment on the first of the month. Friends and church members donated furniture and household items, and he did not mind that the items were used. He treated them as if they were plated with gold.

To this day, the apartment is furnished beautifully and is in a wonderful area just across the street from the university. The area is bustling with activity and has connecting bus lines nearby. Joe has lived in the same apartment for years. I hope he can stay there for many more. Joe stayed on at the college library for several years until the management changed and they could no longer keep volunteers. However, before he could find a new volunteer position, Joe became ill again.

The Heart Again
His heart condition had been under control for many years but the doctor told me that Joe's kidneys and liver were beginning to fail. He was on 11 different medications a day and his body was having some difficulty processing it all. The doctor tried to prepare me by saying, "This is the beginning of the end." Years earlier, when Joe first started taking the heart medication, the doctor told me that at some point, Joe would develop a tolerance and that the medication would no longer work as well. Well, that time was upon us.

The cardiologist increased Joe's medication and required that someone help Joe with his daily chores. She believed taking care of the apartment, doing laundry, and shopping were too much for him. She filled out forms for the Regional Center to obtain assistance for Joe, and his status changed to supported living, requiring someone to help Joe every day.

A new organization with workers who had nursing education

took over. Today at 56 years old, Joe's life is very different. He lives a much quieter life now and needs time to rest between activities. He still has his beautiful apartment in a wonderful area. He has assistance with household needs, attends church services and meetings, and meets with friends on a regular basis. Joe is still in the third stage of congestive heart failure but, at this time, his condition is stable. Joe has lived an interesting life, full of achievements and successes. He has had many mountains to climb. And he has climbed and conquered them beautifully.

Joe's Life
Joe has achieved more than anyone ever expected. That is everyone but me. I know Joe. I know what he was capable of doing and achieving. He has been affirmed in his value as a person and has had a life worth living and filled with opportunities. He has had struggles, yes. But did he ever give up? No. Joe taught me how to forge ahead and take the blows that inevitably come with life. He taught me how to deal with those blows head-on. He taught me that we all have mountains to climb and showed me how to climb them. Joe taught me tolerance and patience. He gave me the opportunity to see differences in people as something of value, taught me to march to a different drumbeat. That has made all the difference in my life.

The Autistic Difference : Middle Adulthood
- *Generativity, ego integrity, feeling good about life---Erikson*

<u>Helping Others</u>
The concept of generativity and of helping others in society is important for the psychological and social development of

autistic middle-aged adults. While many autistic middle-aged adults remain single due to difficulties in developing social relationships, being single does not mean they cannot accomplish a sense of generativity. Many autistic middle-aged adults volunteer in various areas of society.

Technology

Because of their ability to focus on non-interpersonal areas of society, they also have a flair for technology. Since technology expertise is in demand, autistic middle-aged adults can work or volunteer in schools, including elementary, middle, and high schools preparing others for a connected world. Many autistic middle-aged adults also can organize and maintain technology clubs in schools along with teaching tech programs. Most teachers would appreciate the assistance. Autistic adults also work in technology and related companies as consultants and troubleshooters.

The important aspects to consider in helping the autistic middle-aged adult find suitable work, volunteer or paid, are their interest areas.

Autistic middle-aged adults also have the choice of generativity or stagnation, but they more than likely will need assistance or a little nudge. Generativity is worthwhile for autistic middle-aged adults to avoid feelings of despair in the elderly stage.

The Autistic Difference: Middle Adulthood
• Concrete Thinking: Need hands-on activities to learn, trial-and-error problem-solving.
• Abstract Thinking: consequences of decisions into future, drop back to Concrete Thinking when stressed, anxious or ill---Piaget.

Twists and Turns

Life provides curve balls for everyone. However, given the level of anxiety that autistic adults can experience, abstract thinking may not be a consistent advantage for the autistic adult and decision-making assistance may be necessary. Considering options in a concrete manner may be more helpful for the autistic middle-aged adult, such as writing lists to explain the pros and cons of an activity or event. If parents are elderly and/or incapable of this assistance, siblings, cousins, longtime friends, enlisted volunteers, or professionals can be authorized to provide help. Th is type of provision can be included in a trust or legal agreement to safeguard autistic adults and allow trusted individuals to act on their behalf so that they may comfortably enter their elder years.

Self-esteem, Self-Worth---Cooley

It is imperative to remain vigilant and resourceful. As autistic children grow into adulthood, we naturally want to let go of the ties that bind them to us giving them wings to fly, to live their own lives in the best way possible. However, parents involvement with adult children, assisting them with tasks that are difficult for them to accomplish but in subtle ways without taking over their lives is vital. They know they are loved, not a burden.

Needs Based Motivation---Maslow

Identify services that are available at the state, county, and city level to assist autistic adult children with things parents can no longer provide.

Law offices that specialize in elder law and disability law can assist in developing needed safeguards for our autistic adults.

Abilities Based Motivation---Bandura

Every adult has a set of skills and abilities, autistic adults included. Using services to enhance abilities will ensure a productive life for autistic adults.

Section Three

The Future

CHAPTER 16

The Brighter Future

Tech Fest

A Much Needed Dash

"It seems that for success in science and art, a dash of autism is essential. The necessary ingredient may be an ability to turn away from the everyday world, to rethink a subject with originality so as to create in new untrodden ways." – Hans Asperger, who identified autism in 1944.

Thoughts on the Present and Future of the Autistic Individual

The future for autistic people is brighter than ever. Research on autism, technology, and social media are helping autistic individuals have better life experiences. Our children are our future. This has always been true, and it will always be true. In this fact lies the hope of the future, and I am hopeful.

Considering that I have been in education for over 40 years, I have seen generations of children become adults and take their place in society and in the world. As an educator, it has been my main focus to assist my students, whether special needs and at-risk or not, to recognize and be motivated to reach the potential that quietly lies within them. I see my role as a teacher not so much as someone who imparts information but as someone who inspires my students to learn and become the people they were meant to be.

Recognition of Individuality
"Everybody is a genius. But if you judge a fish by its ability to climb a tree, it will live its whole life believing it is stupid." – Albert Einstein

Our world is ever-changing, and that is as it should be. Technology and new research into autism has fueled changes in the diagnosis and education of autistic children. There has been incredible progress in helping special needs children reach their potential. The one reality that has not changed for autistic children is that parents and teachers need to view each autistic child as an individual and to encourage and nurture their individual abilities and interests. This is vital if the autistic child is to more easily benefit from what school and society have to offer. The understanding of the autistic child as an individual is still the number one most important factor in assisting the child in developing his/her potential.

The information gleaned from technology and research cannot replace the personal knowledge that parents and teachers have regarding the autistic child, and they best work in conjunction with that knowledge to benefit the child. In this same vein, personal observation and knowledge of the child is vital for early diagnosis of autism.

Research has proven that the earlier the diagnosis, the earlier therapeutic treatment begins, the better the results. A possibility exists that autism will have a lesser impact on children's lives in the near future. Certainly, as a society, we know more now about the signs and symptoms of autism than we did in the past.

School Services
Early diagnosis also allows for early assistance through school districts. By federal law, schools must offer services and treatment to children as young as three years old. Early treatment helps a child step out of his/her private world into the outside world at a much earlier age. It is your right as a parent to take advantage of these federal and state laws that are in place to assist parents of autistic children in acquiring early treatment and services that increase the likelihood of success in school.

Regular public school classroom teachers are required to take at least one course in special education practices while preparing for their teaching credentials. Considering the number and different types of learning disabilities and levels of autism, one or even two courses in special education may not be enough for teachers who can have several special needs students in their mainstream classrooms. As research develops new treatments for special needs children, teachers need ongoing Professional Development regarding the best practices to assist their students. Interestingly, research has shown that special needs students perform better in regular classrooms than they do solely in special needs classes. As a result, many school districts are providing special needs students their services in regular classrooms. The result has been improved test scores for special needs students while there has been no negative impact on regular education students. A win-win. It also would be advantageous for new teachers to consider studying special education along with regular education practices. With funding an issue, some school districts across the country are not in compliance with federal and state education laws. This is problematic as children and teachers alike are not receiving the proper amount of support required for educating special needs children.

The concept of further educating teachers with respect to special needs children should be expanded to provide parental education on signs and symptoms of autism, and other special needs along with behavior pattern treatments such as *Applied Behavior Analysis and Therapy,* that are known to assist special needs children.

Technology has changed every aspect of our society, including the classroom. Teaching and student practice programs abound. Reading, math, science, and social studies programs are available to assist teachers with difficult to learn concepts for their students. While some question the use of so much technology in the classroom, others realize that computer use for autistic and other special needs students has been incredibly beneficial, and they seem to excel when using computers for learning, practicing, writing, and research. Multiple research studies have shown that reading and writing on computers, tablets, and other electronic devices use a different part of the brain than when that same activity is accomplished with paper and pencil. This difference seems to be an advantage for autistic students. While the fast pace of technology may frustrate parents and teachers, the advance of technology in education has been a benefit for autistic and other special needs students.

When planning for college, parents should consider other factors besides their child's abilities. Financial responsibilities must be weighed. There are many options for students with special needs. Federal and state grants are available, and information regarding these grants can be obtained from high school counselors. Private grants and scholarships are also available. Online research can present much information on these scholarships. Consider a community college for general education requirements as it is less expensive than a 4-year college. Colleges now have *Success Centers* to assist special needs students so the choice of colleges has broadened providing parents and students with more options.

Social Media
Social media can be an especially positive experience for autistic and other special needs children and adolescents. Because autistic individuals tend to reside in their own mental worlds, social media can provide a very necessary outlet for social development where they can seek out specific connections based on their interests.

Autistic children and teens seem to thrive with the opportunities that online gaming provides and many autistic teens excel at it. They can develop friendships and long-term relationships online, where no eye contact is needed. They finally can develop longed-for friendships.

However, social media also poses special dangers about which parents and teachers need to be aware. Sexual predators, scam artists, among others, lurk in online chat rooms and gaming arenas.

These dangers are real for special needs and non-special needs children alike. The younger the child, the greater the danger. Consistent monitoring by parents and teachers is vital for the safety of young people surfing the internet and developing online friendships and relationships. Research parental guides for new safety monitoring programs for home and school computers and tablets. Technology is a gift for autistic children and teens but learning to use it wisely is important. When managed with common sense, social media can be a terrific outlet for autistic children, teens, and adults. Easier said than done but important to accomplish.

Technology/STEM
Because autistic individuals perceive the world somewhat differently, science, technology, engineering, and math (STEM) are areas in which many autistic individuals excel, and the career field in STEM is growing. Nurture the interests in these areas as job opportunities can develop into careers for autistic teens and adults. In the future, autistic men and women might be in high demand to take up jobs and careers in technology that others cannot understand, nor fulfill.

Health Issues and Living Longer
Autistic and other special needs individuals are living longer than previous generations due to modern health care advances, and parents are likely to be faced with the needs of autistic adults and autistic elderly. Health care professionals need to be aware that their autistic patients may not be able to thoroughly explain their symptoms. Doctors and other health professionals also need to be aware of the characteristics of elderly individuals with special needs who are prone to health conditions such as hypertension, anxiety, digestive disorders, and sleep disorders. Medicare and Social Security may well need to be expanded as more special

needs people live well into old age.

Parents need to consider the laws and policies in their states so that their autistic children will receive proper care in their old age. Many states provide for the opportunity to establish *Special Needs Trusts*, and it's important to put as many safeguards as possible in place for the aging autistic individual.

The future can indeed be bright for autistic children as they grow and develop, especially as the ongoing research into autism progresses. Technology is providing many new possibilities for autistic teens and adults, and they seem to understand it better than anyone else. **Perhaps now more than ever, our autistic children are our future.**

Chapter 17

There is No Such Thing as a Purple Horse

People Who Changed the World

"Great spirits have always encountered opposition from mediocre minds. The mediocre mind is incapable of understanding the man who refuses to bow blindly to conventional prejudice and chooses instead to express his opinions courageously and honestly." Albert Einstein

It was a bright sunny spring day in Chicago. I was about 10 years old and sitting in my overcrowded classroom. The teacher was explaining a Friday afternoon art project. While listening to her, I was gazing at a tree with tiny purple flowers just outside the window. When the teacher asked us to start drawing, I began to draw a horse, a purple horse the very shade of purple on the tiny flowers of the tree outside my classroom window. As she walked around the classroom, she commented on the students' drawings. As she approached my desk, she paused asking what I was drawing. I replied, "A purple horse." Disdainfully, she emphatically said, "There is no such thing as a purple horse." She, then, took my drawing ripping it to pieces muttering, "Stop dreaming and start over with something real this time." I felt ashamed of "dreaming" and just sat quietly for a few minutes trying to think of something to draw. Being fascinated by the purple flowers, I wanted a purple horse but apparently, I couldn't have one. So, I drew a purple tree. Unfortunately, that did not go so well with the teacher either. I guess she hadn't looked out the window.

Over the years, I have thought about that incident and its impact on me. I realized it caused me to suppress my creativity in order to fit in, to be less of a problem, and to be accepted. As I grew older, gaining more experience about myself and the world, I questioned why there could not be a purple horse. Why couldn't there be purple trees or purple people, for that matter? Just why couldn't I be different and draw a purple horse? Why couldn't people be different?

I wanted a purple horse or at least have the freedom to draw one if I chose to do so. Then, one day, when I least expected it, I found my purple horse. My son, Joe was born. From the very first, he was different. As he grew, I realized he was intelligent, creative, caring, courageous, and *different*. He was purple in a black and white world.

The teacher who admonished me, "There's no such thing as a purple horse" was mistaken. Completely mistaken. Throughout history, there have been people who were different. People, who, initially were ignored, berated, ostracized or worse just for being different. However, throughout history, people who were/are different had the imagination and creativity to change the world!

We study these people in history classes. We honor them for what they have created. We rarely discuss the struggles they endured while growing up. But we should. We should honor their courage and tenacity for continuing to create despite the courage and tenacity for continuing to create despite the adversity they experienced.

Many of the people who changed the world were/are on the *autism spectrum.* They saw/see the world differently, therefore, they were able to create in ways most of us find unimaginable. In his 84 years, **Thomas Alva Edison** acquired an amazing 1,093 patents (singly or jointly) and helped develop the phonograph, the incandescent light bulb, and one of the earliest motion picture cameras. He also created the world's first industrial research laboratory. Thomas Edison was a poor student. When a school principal called Edison, "addled" his mother was furious, took him out of the school, and taught him at home. Edison said many years later, "My mother was the making of me." He was imaginative and inquisitive, but, because most instruction was through memorization and he had difficulty hearing, he was bored and was labeled a misfit.

Albert Einstein developed the theory of relativity which revolutionized our understanding of space, time, gravity, and the universe. Being slow to develop verbally, he became curious about abstract concepts - such as space and time. His father gave him a compass when he was five, and he became interested in the nature of magnetic fields for the rest of his life. He preferred to think in pictures rather than words. Given some of the difficulties he had as a child, some researchers believe Einstein to have been on the autism spectrum. Simon Baron-Cohen, the director of the autism research center at Cambridge University, is among those. He writes that autism is associated with a, "Particularly intense drive to systemize and organize."

Considered to be on the autism spectrum, **Steve Jobs** preferred doing things by himself. He showed an early interest in electronics and computers. He spent quite a bit of time in the garage workshop of a neighbor who worked at Hewlett-Packard. When he joined the Hewlett-Packard Explorer Club, he observed engineers demonstrate new products. He saw his first computer at twelve and was hooked and immediately knew that he wanted to work with computers.

Greta Thunberg was diagnosed with *Asperger Syndrome*, which is on the *autism spectrum*. Wanting to make a greater impact on lawmakers to address climate change. Greta Thunberg, for almost three weeks prior to the Swedish election in September 2018, missed school to sit outside the country's parliament with a sign that read, "School Strike for Climate." Alone for the first day of the strike, she was, then, joined each subsequent day by more and more people. Her story gained international attention. She inspired hundreds of thousands of students around the world to participate in their own related projects.

Satoshi Tajiri is a Japanese video game designer best known for creating Nintendo's Pokémon. He is also on the autism spectrum. As a child, he enjoyed collecting insects as a hobby, which became the inspiration for his video games. Children who knew him called him, "Dr. Bug." He attended a two-year technical degree program at Tokyo National College of Technology majoring in electronics and computer science.

Each one of the above-mentioned people were/are considered, "different." Each was considered to likely be or was diagnosed to be on the autism spectrum. Our autistic children are different, yes. But consider, is your student a budding Einstein?, Edison?, Jobs?, Thunberg?, or Tajiri?

Autistic children often are "round pegs" in a "square world." Parents and teachers would love to erase the struggles children on the spectrum endure. Given that we really don't understand the cause of autism, the "cure" is elusive. But do we want them to be "cured" or do we want to lessen the struggle? Do we want to change the way they function to "fit in" or do we want to make functioning in our world easier for them? Do we want to change the way they see the world, or do we want to see the world through their eyes?

These are vital questions as autism comes with aspects causing difficulties (such as social interaction) AND aspects of awesome abilities (such as photographic memory).

As a mother, teacher, and school psychologist, I would love to see the struggles end. But ending the struggle is not in the human experience. Lessening struggle is more realistic. My dream is to have parents, teachers, counselors, therapists, and school psychologists focus more on the awesome aspects of autism as the world needs the creative point of view these individuals hold. Autistic children and adults see the world differently, experience the world differently. Because our autistic children see the world differently, they help us to see the world differently. **IF** we let them. By allowing our children to change **our** world, our autistic children CAN and WILL change the **rest** of the world.

Epilogue

"...I took the road less traveled by and that has made all the difference." ~ Robert Frost

People help people. This is perhaps the most important connection in life. We depend upon it. Each of us has experiences we can use to help others. We all have stories to tell. It really doesn't matter if we succeeded or failed. Regardless, our story has value. If we have succeeded, others can use the same tactics we used. If we have failed, ideally others will learn from us and not do the same thing. Learning from our mistakes is actually a magnificent way to learn.

When I considered writing this book, I thought, "Who the heck am I to write a book about our story? Would anyone care? Would our story really help anyone?"

Then I thought of an episode of the popular TV show, *The West Wing*. In this particular episode, John, the chief of staff and a recovering alcoholic, tries to help another staff member struggling with a similar problem. The other staff member balks at the help, saying that John doesn't know what he's really going through. John considers his point and proceeds to tell the other staff member a story.

I call it "The Hole Story," and it goes something like this: "There was a man who was walking along a sidewalk and because he was thinking of other things, he didn't notice a deep and dangerous hole. He fell into it. Unfortunately, try as he might, he couldn't seem to find a way out of the hole. He tried to climb out. No ladder, no rocks to climb on. He looked for an exit deep in the hole. There was none that he could find. He called out hoping that someone would come by and hear him. And someone did. First, a doctor came by. Hearing the man call out, he looked into the hole and realized that the man was stuck in the hole. The doctor, being concerned for the well-being of the man, wrote out a prescription and handed it to him, telling him to fill it as soon as he got out of the hole.

Next, a lawyer came along and, because of the man's yelling, looked into the hole and realized the man was stuck. The lawyer, also concerned, handed the trapped man his business card telling him to contact him when he got out of the hole. The lawyer said that he wanted to help the man sue the people responsible for creating the hole. The lawyer walked away just as the doctor had.

Soon, a priest came along, heard the man's calls, and approached the hole. He heard the man's story and after some thought, the priest said he would pray for the man to find a way out of the hole and he, too, walked away.

The trapped man, feeling despondent, was about to give up when one of his friends saw him in the hole. The friend approached the man and asked him what had happened. The man told his friend that he was trapped in this hole and could not get out. The friend listened and then said he would help and proceeded to do the unthinkable. He jumped into the hole with his friend. Well, you can imagine!

The trapped man was distraught and angry. He told his friend that he must be an idiot because now they were both stuck in the hole. His friend looked at him, shook his head and quietly said, 'I've been in this hole before. I know the way out.' And the man's friend, with patience and caring, showed the man the way out of the deep and dangerous hole."

I guess that sums up the reason I decided to write our story.

Epilogue

Joe and I have been in a deep and dangerous hole at times, and we figured the way out - or at least we figured *our* way out. This book is the story of what I learned crawling out of the hole. My hope is that our story will help teachers assist parents and students to climb out of their deep and dangerous hole and find their way to a beautiful, happy, and rewarding life.

Printed in the USA
CPSIA information can be obtained
at www.ICGtesting.com
LVHW091447060524
779122LV00004B/344